I0504988

BABY TURTLE MUKBANG COLORING BOOK
By Valeriia Laryoshyna

First paperback edition May 2023

Book design by Valeriia Laryoshyna

ISBN: 9798394363092

Published by Kindle Direct Publishing

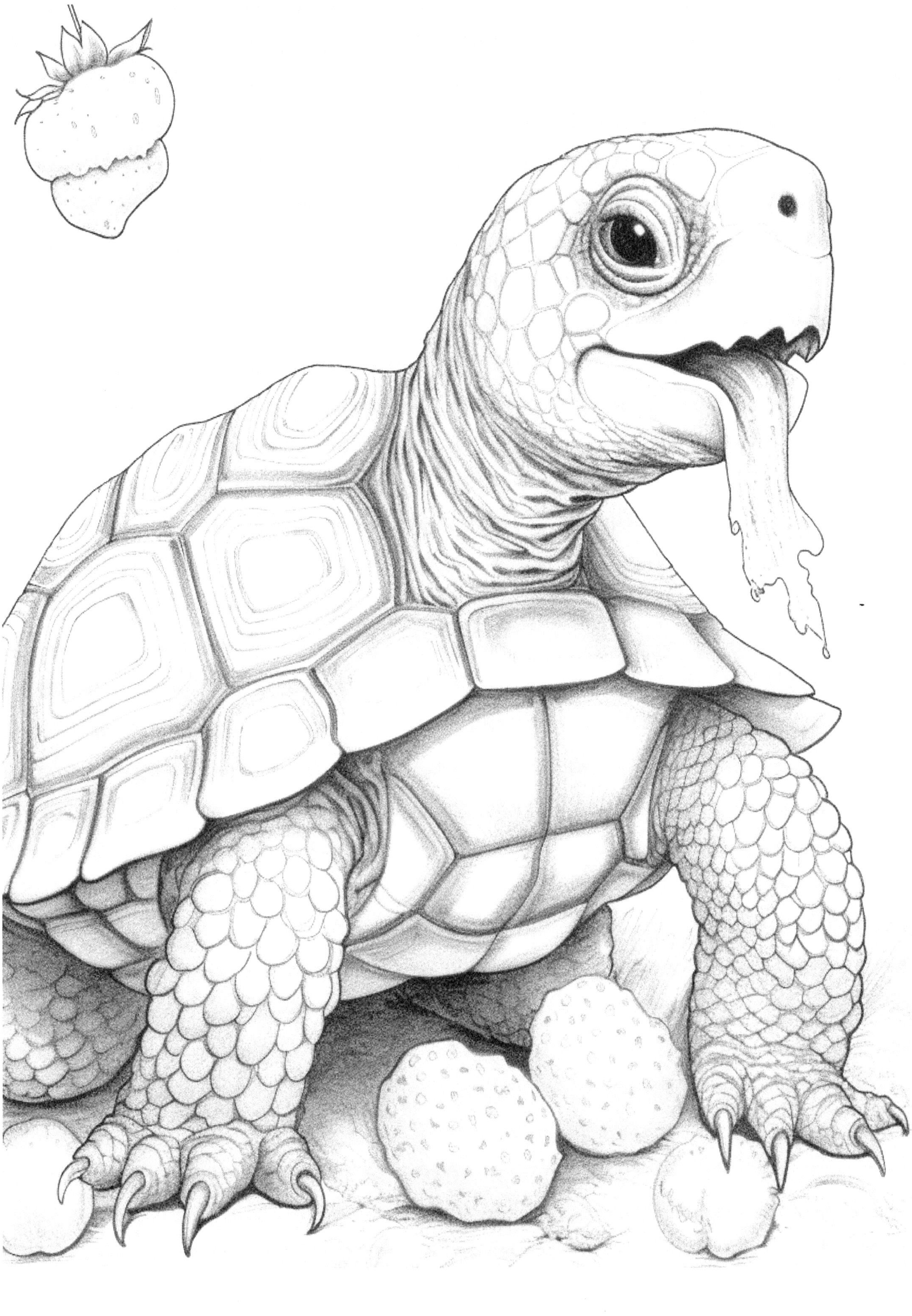

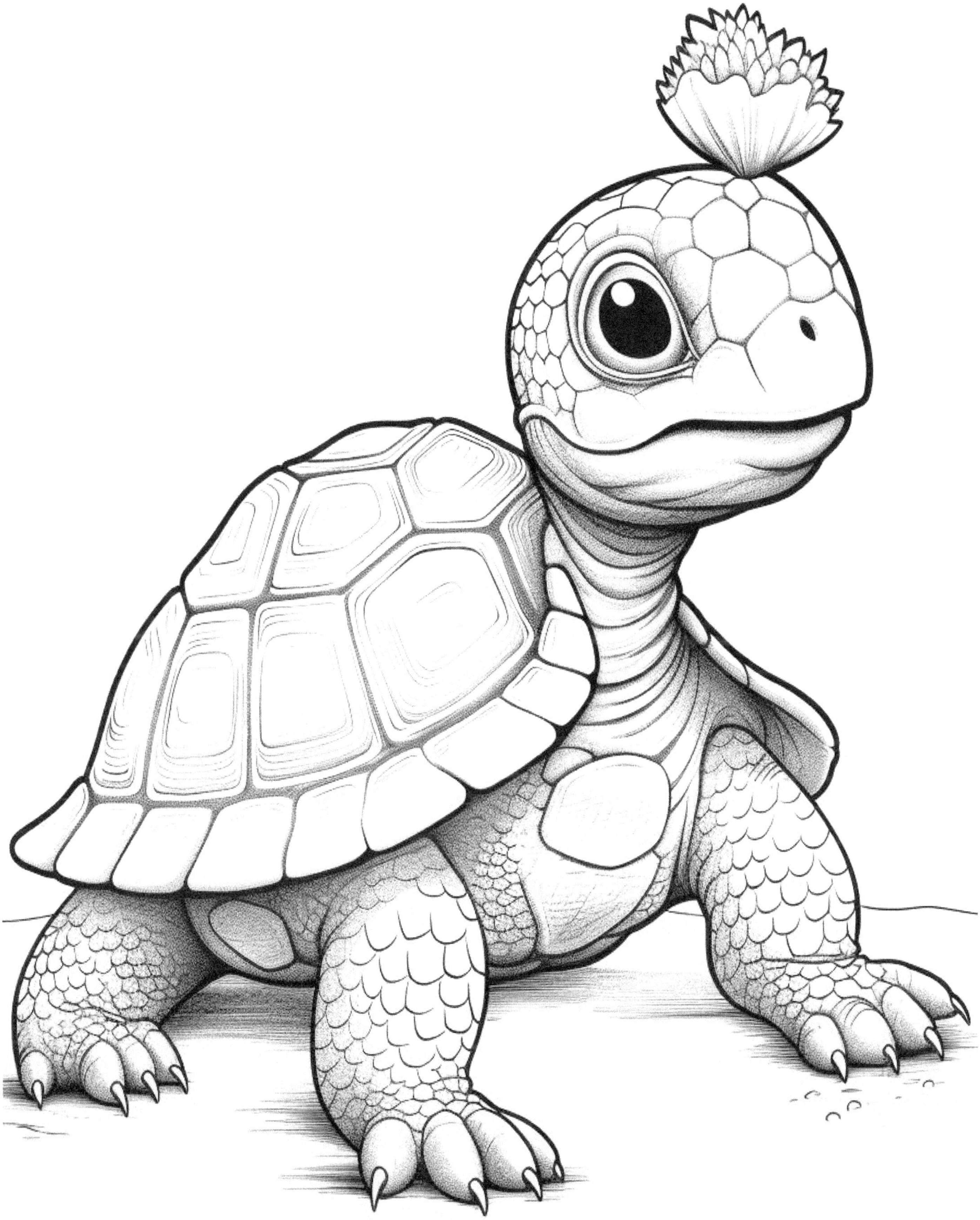

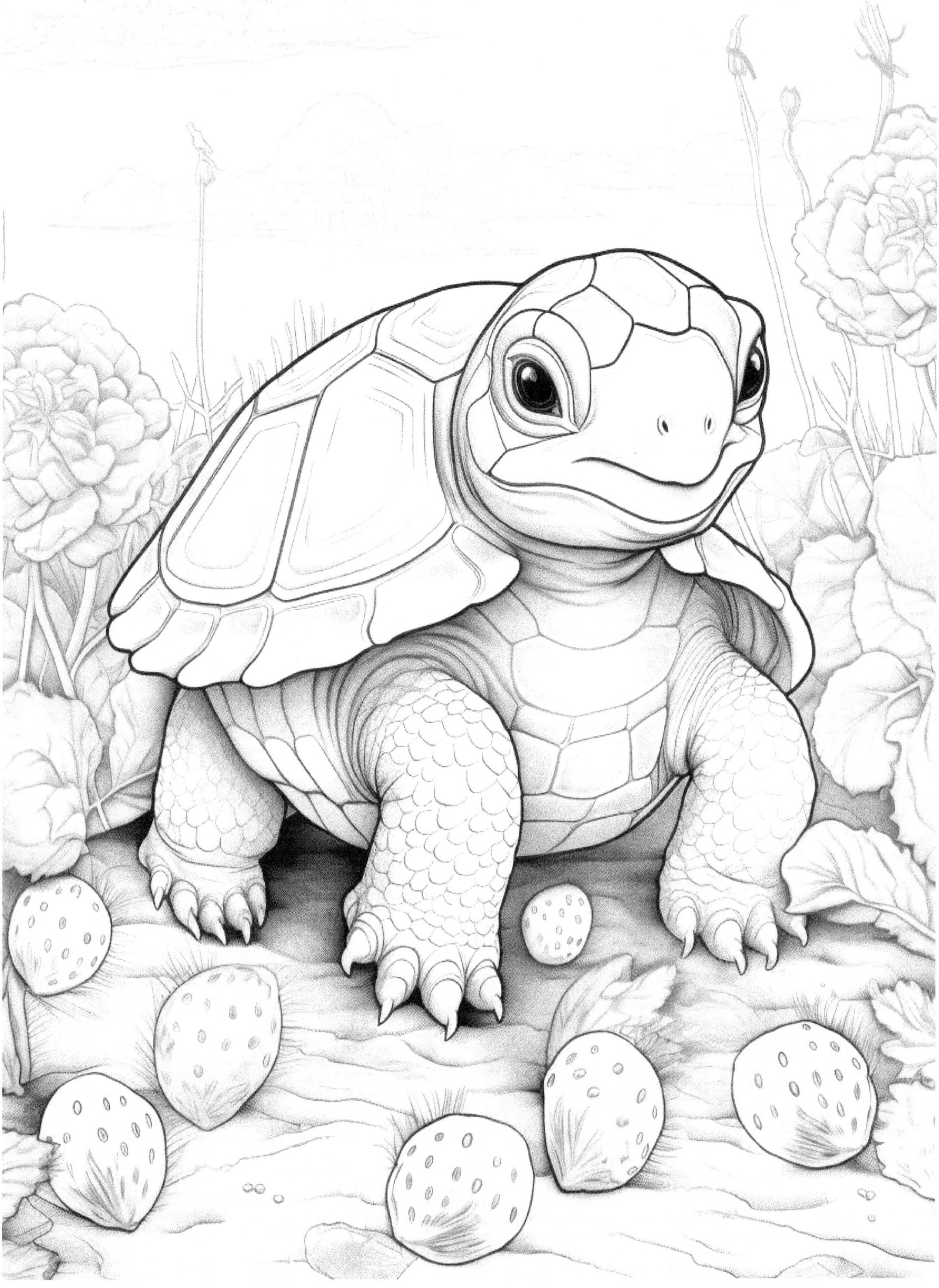

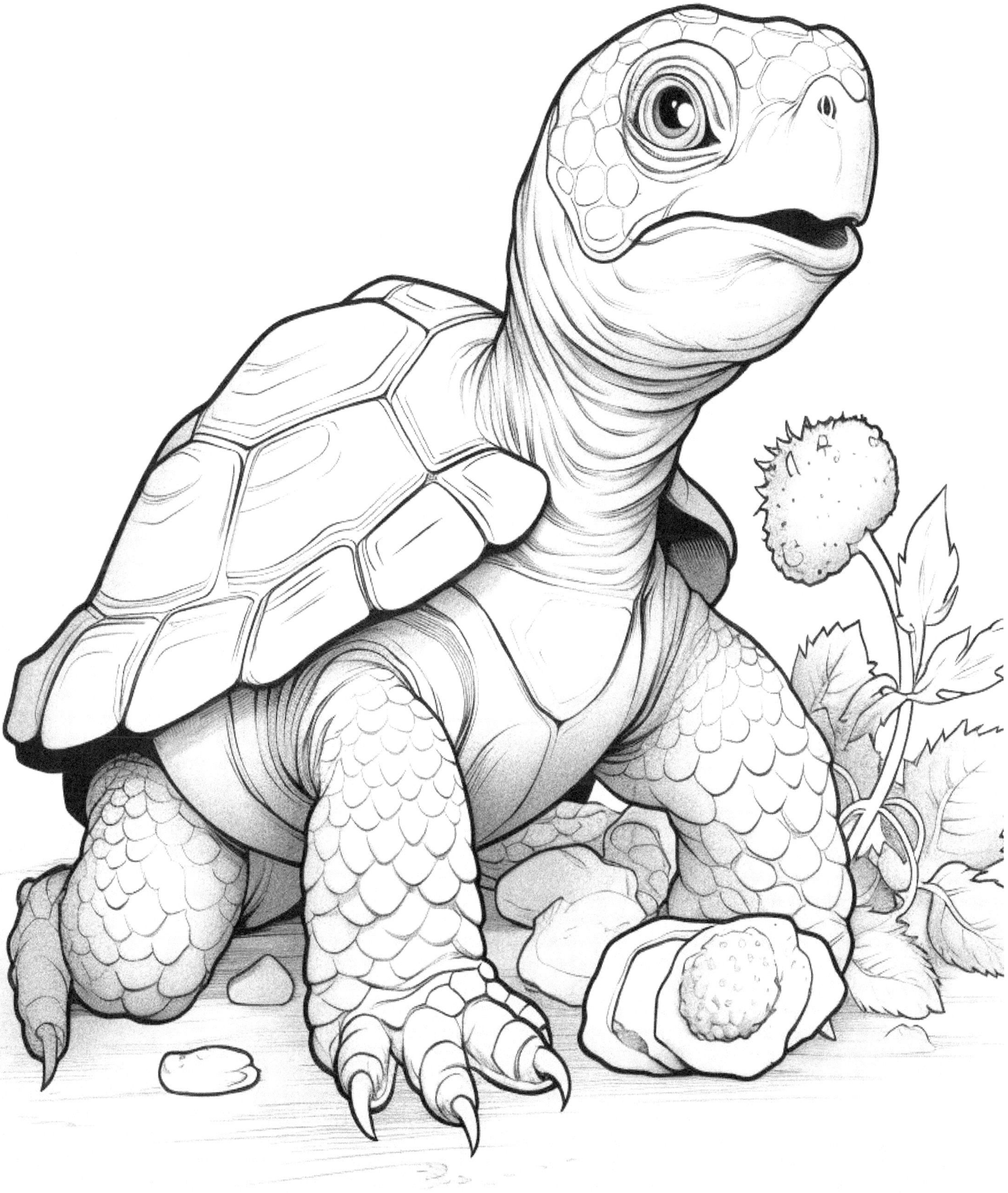

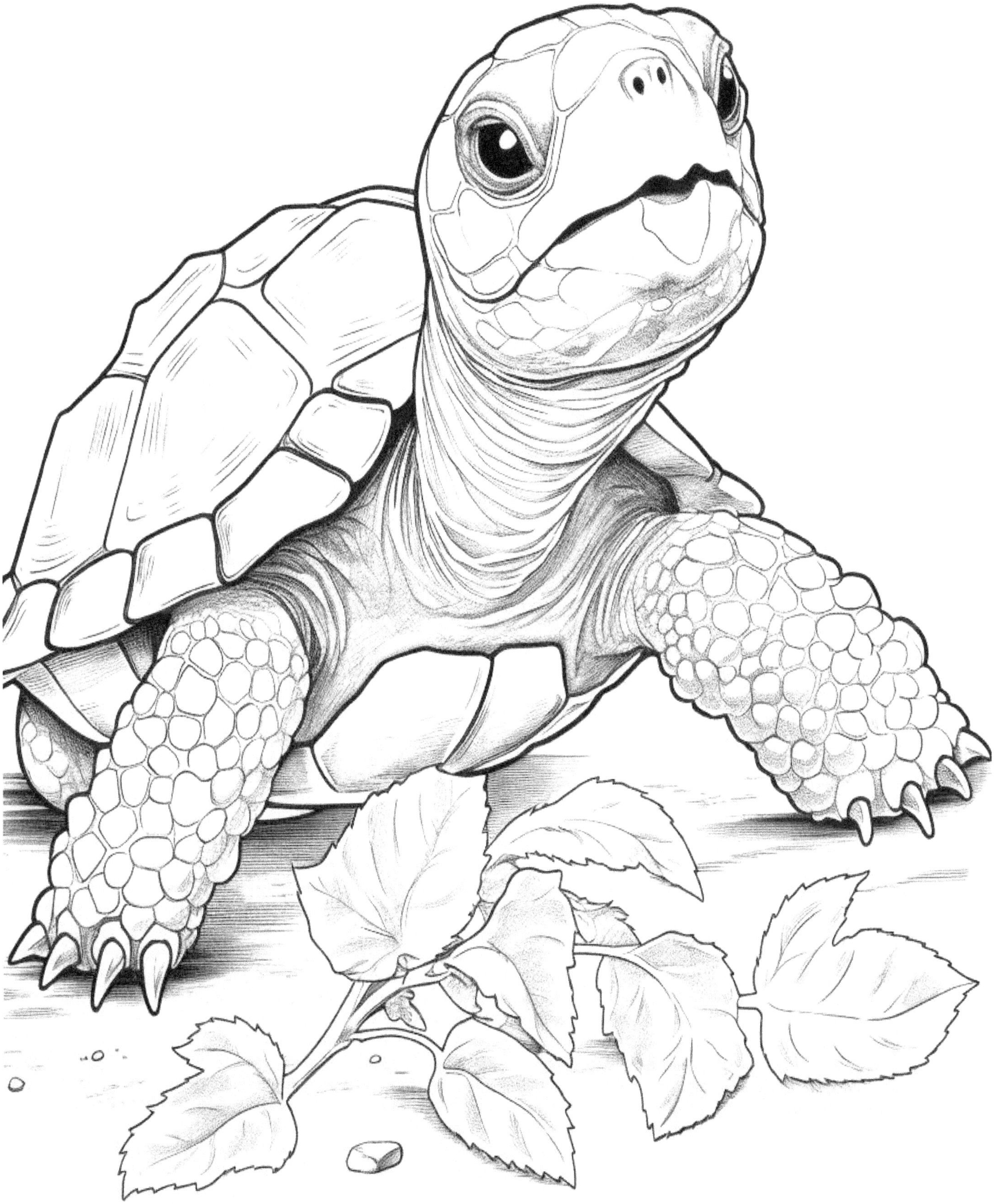

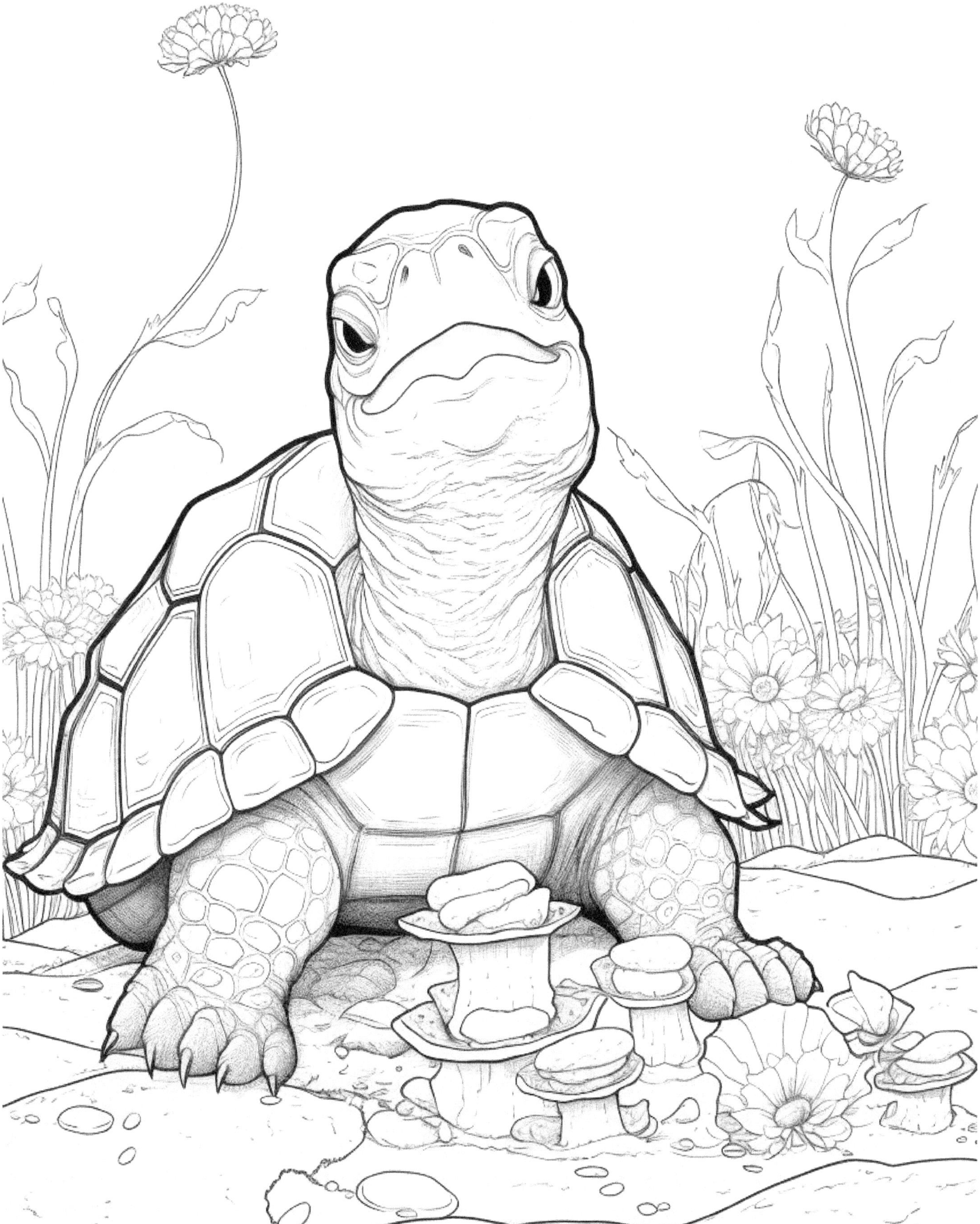

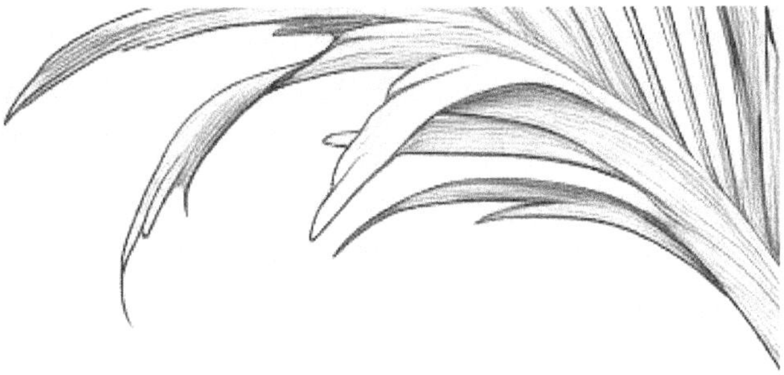

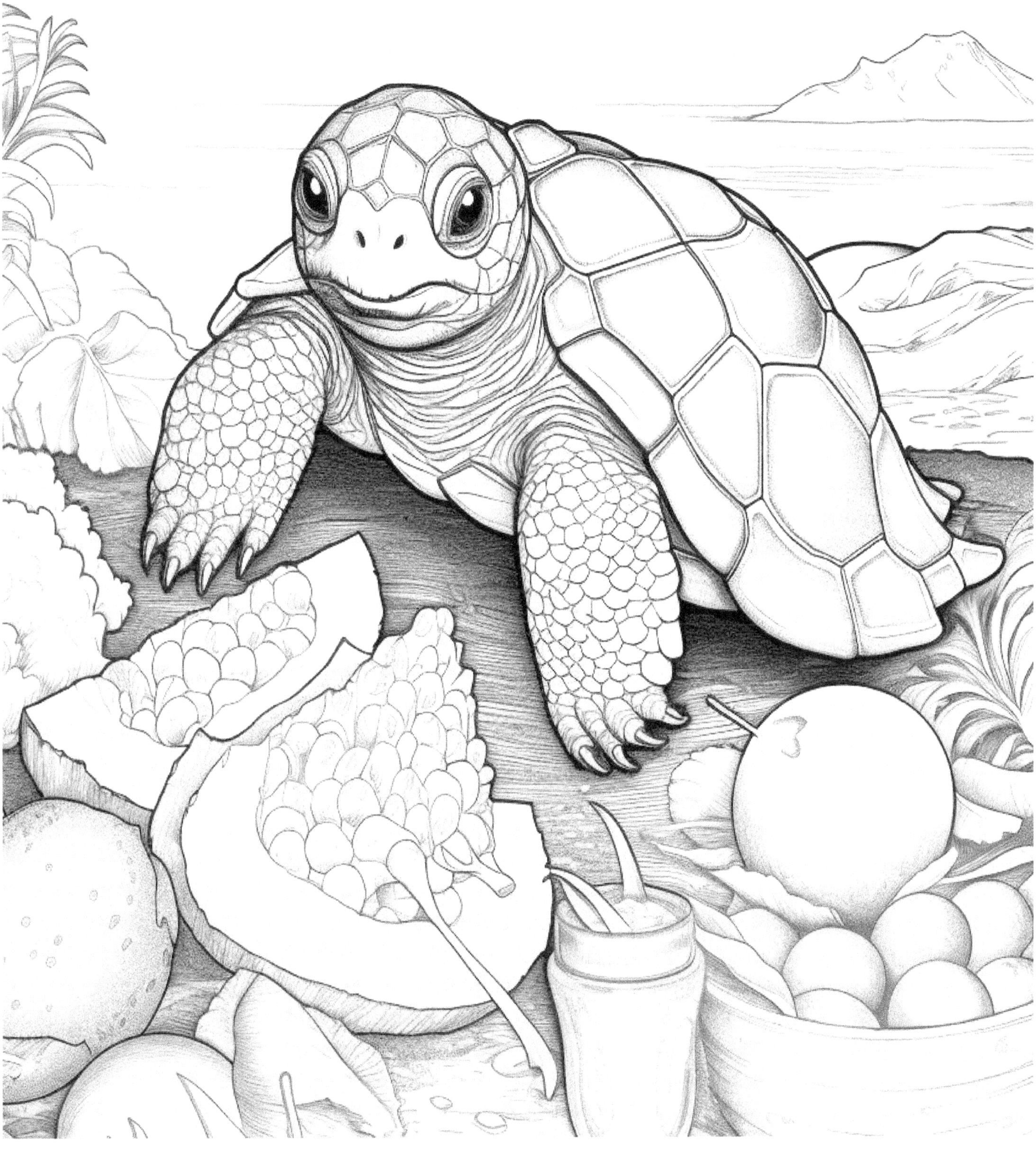

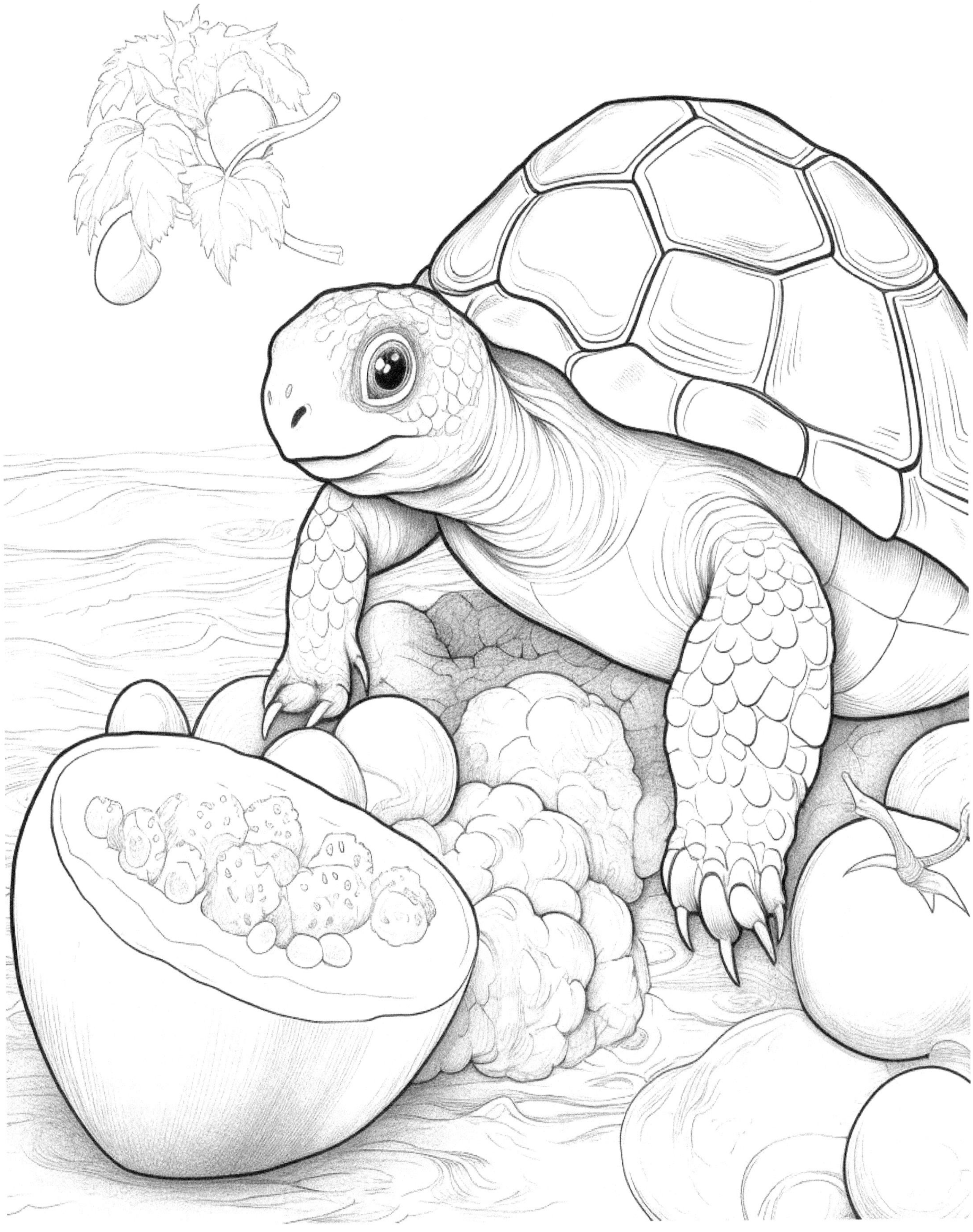

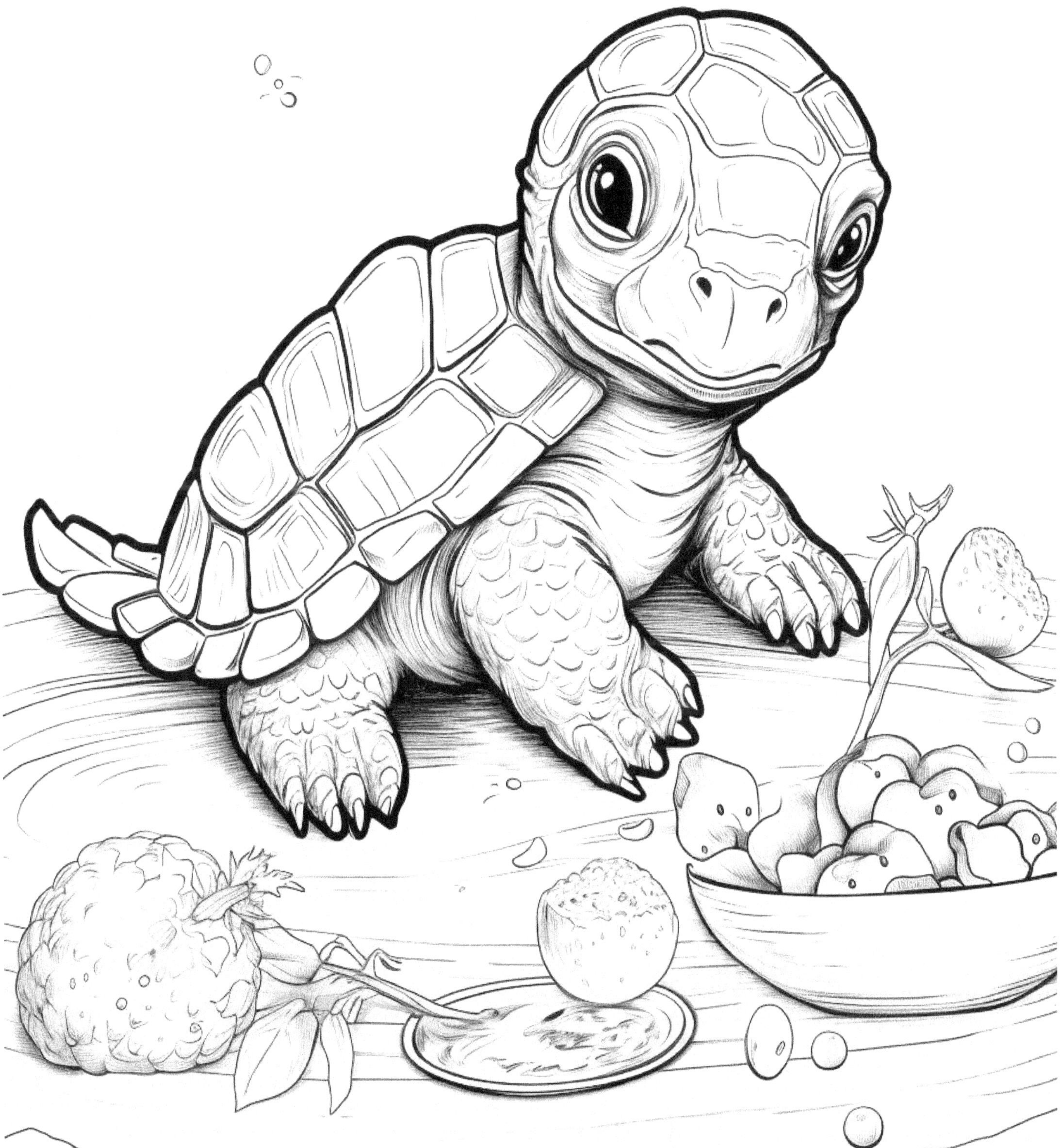

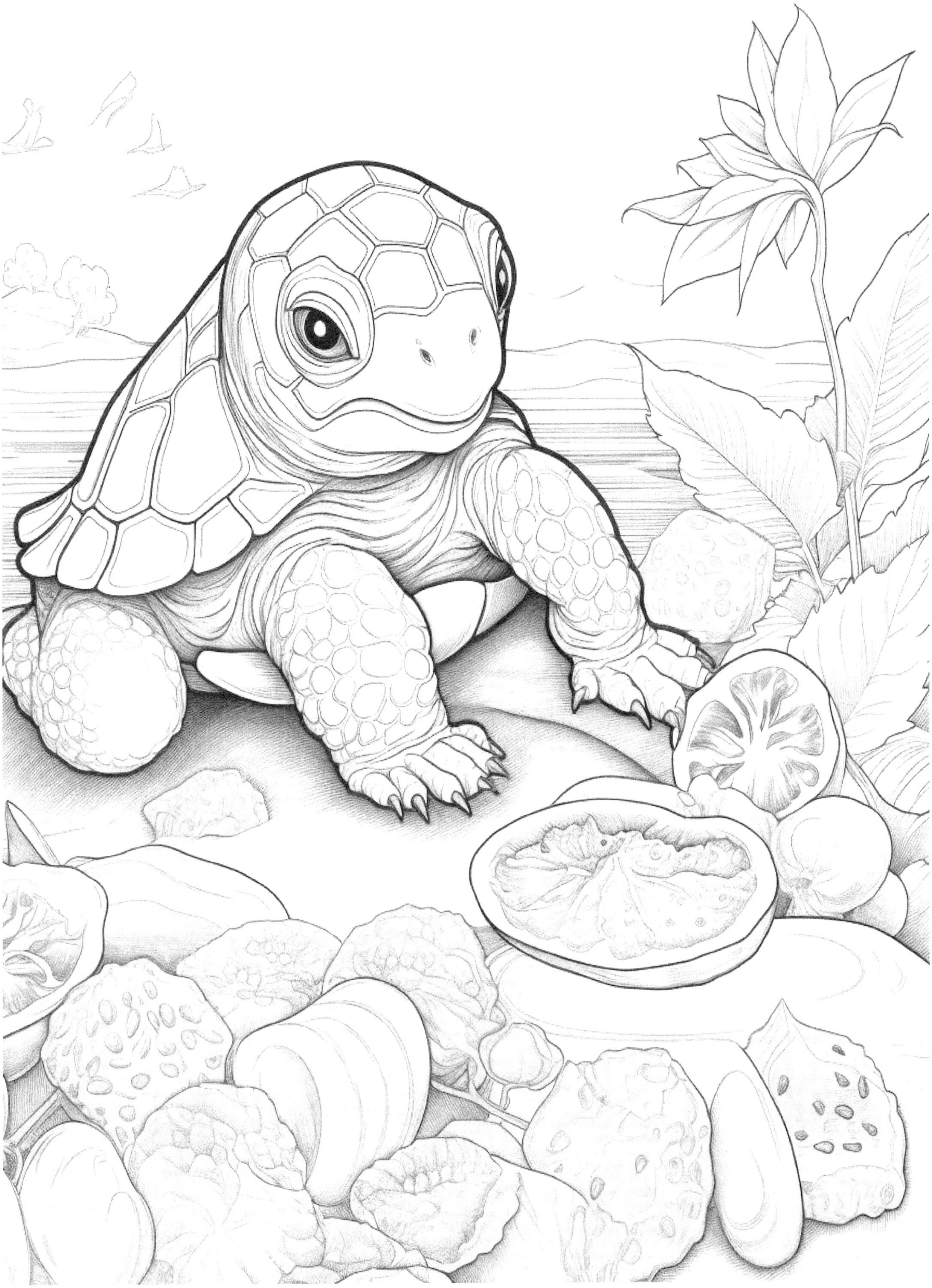

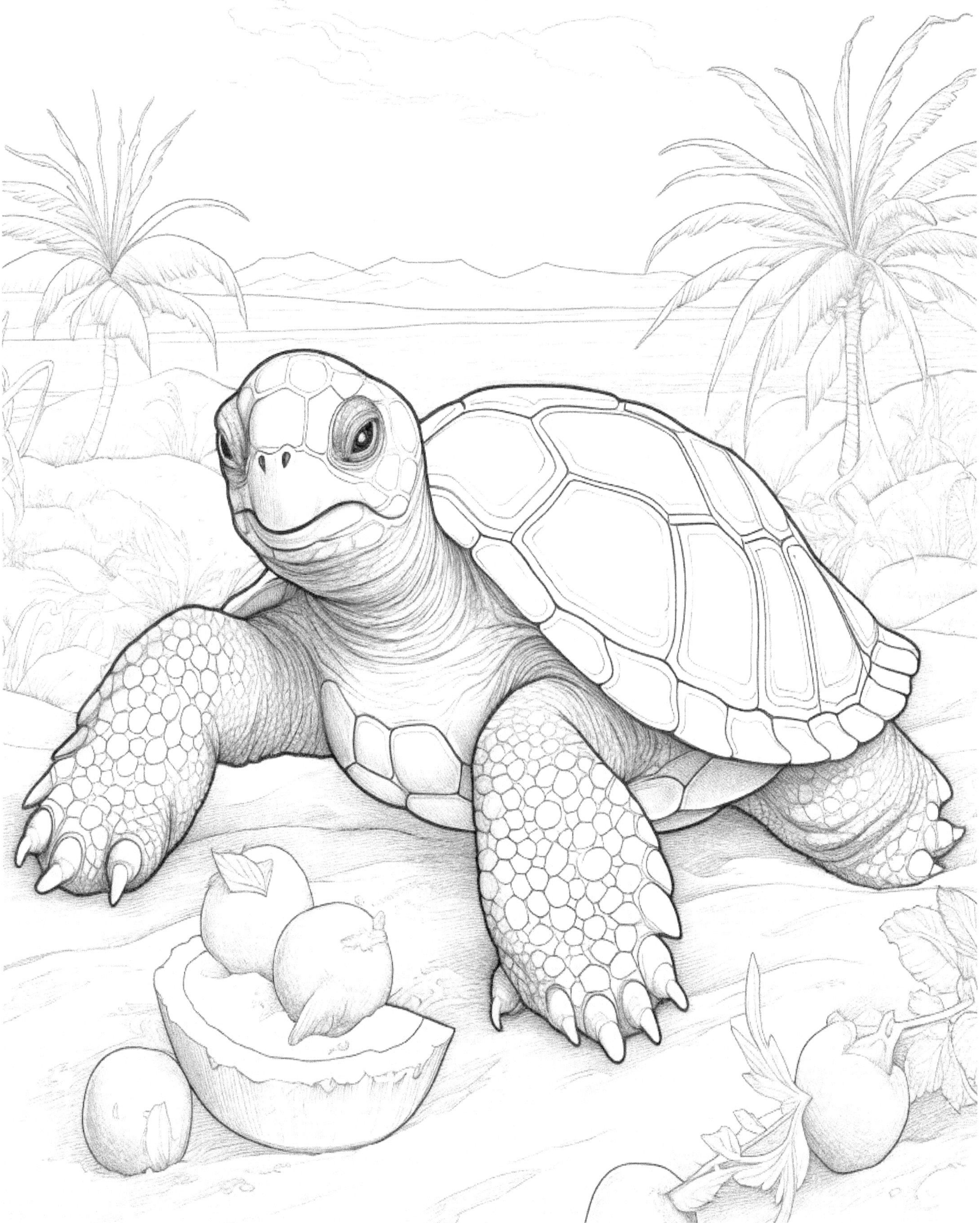

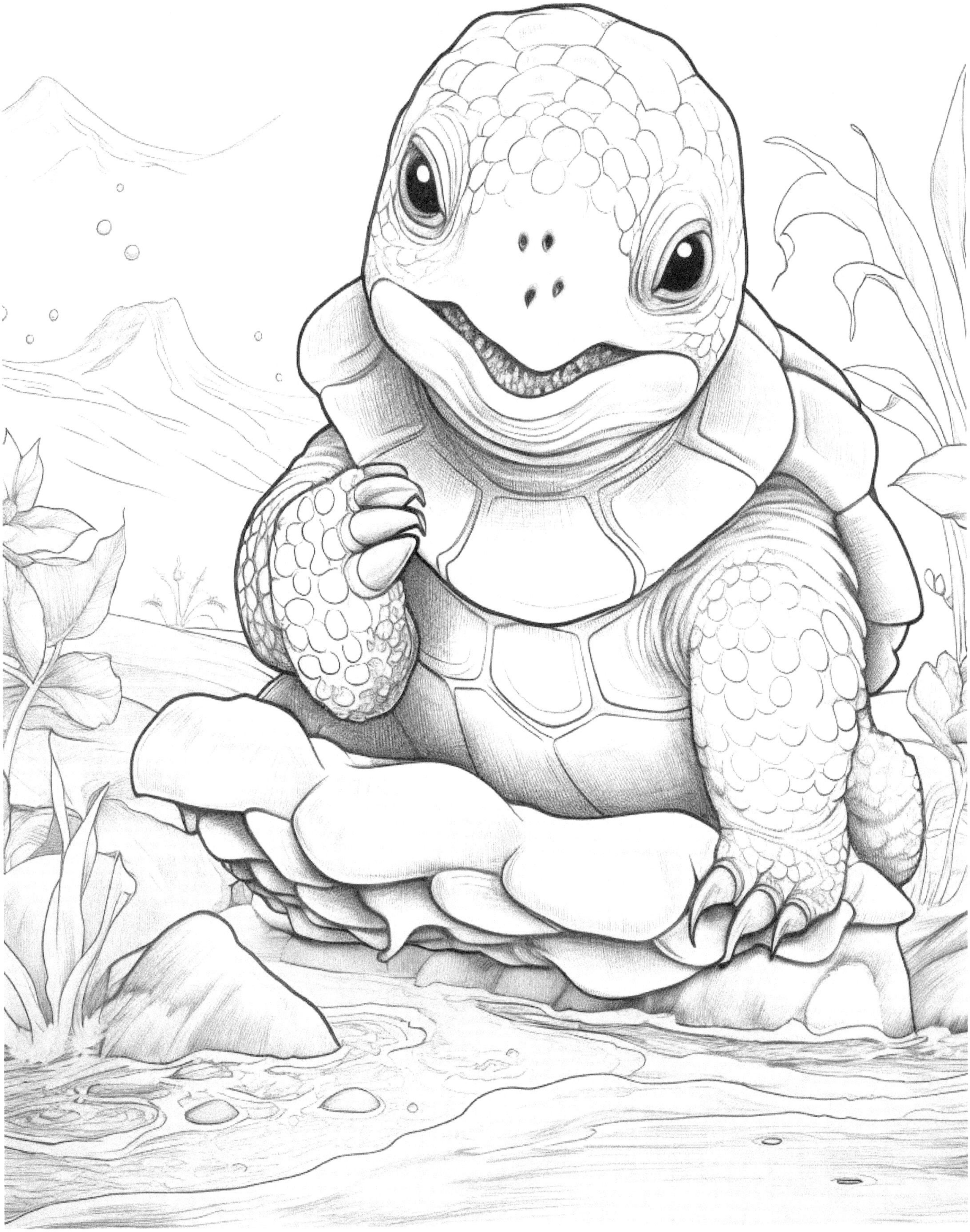

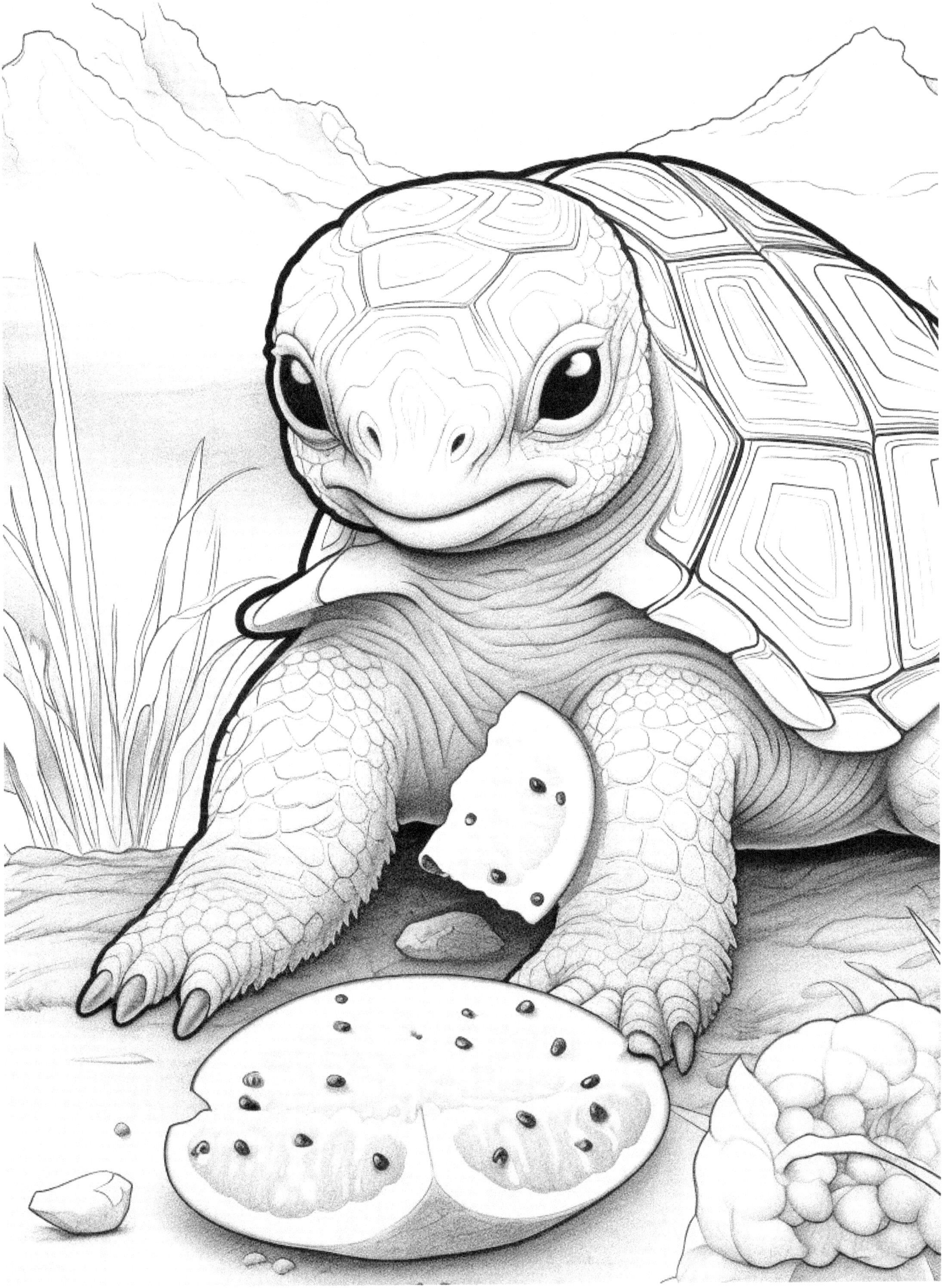

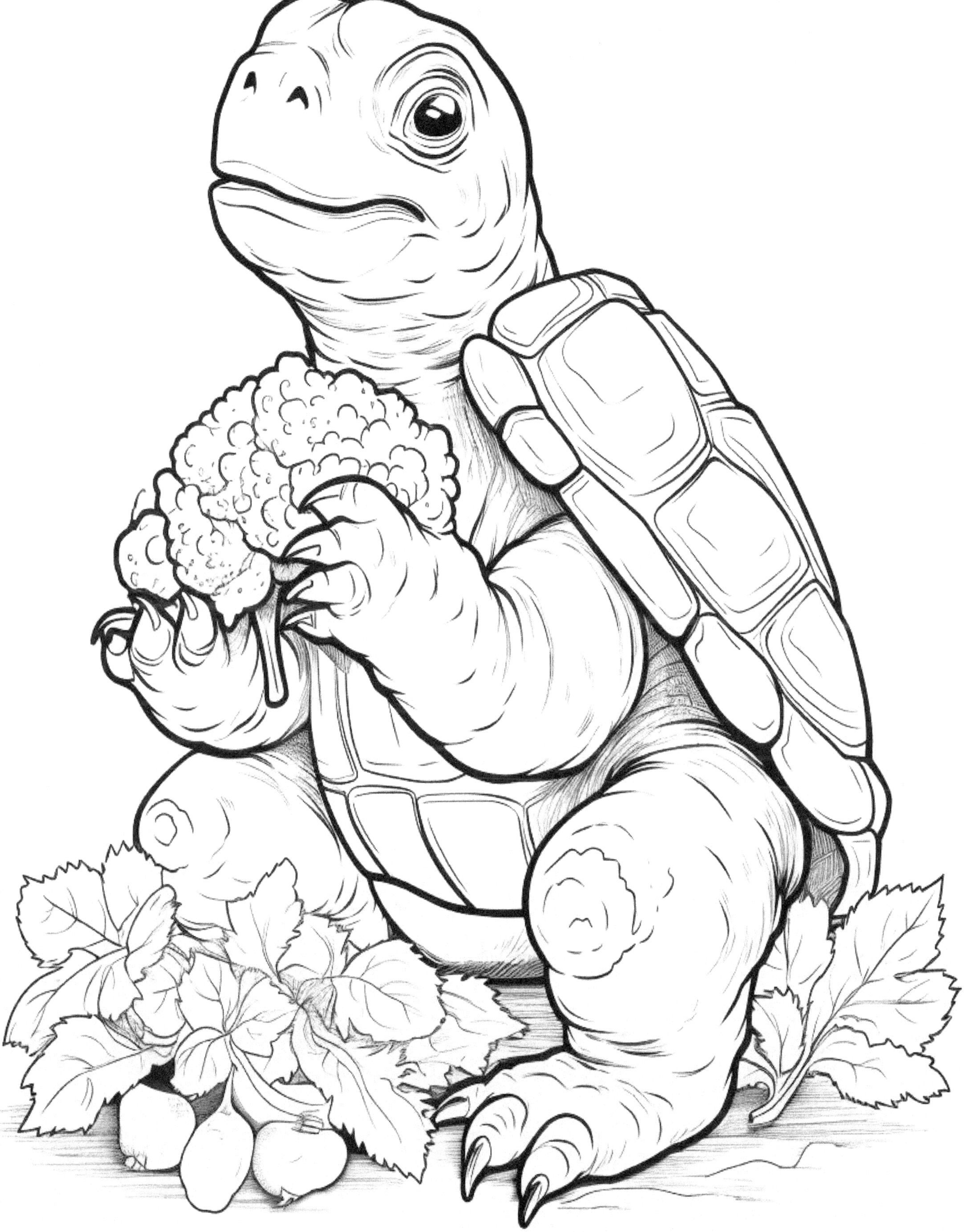

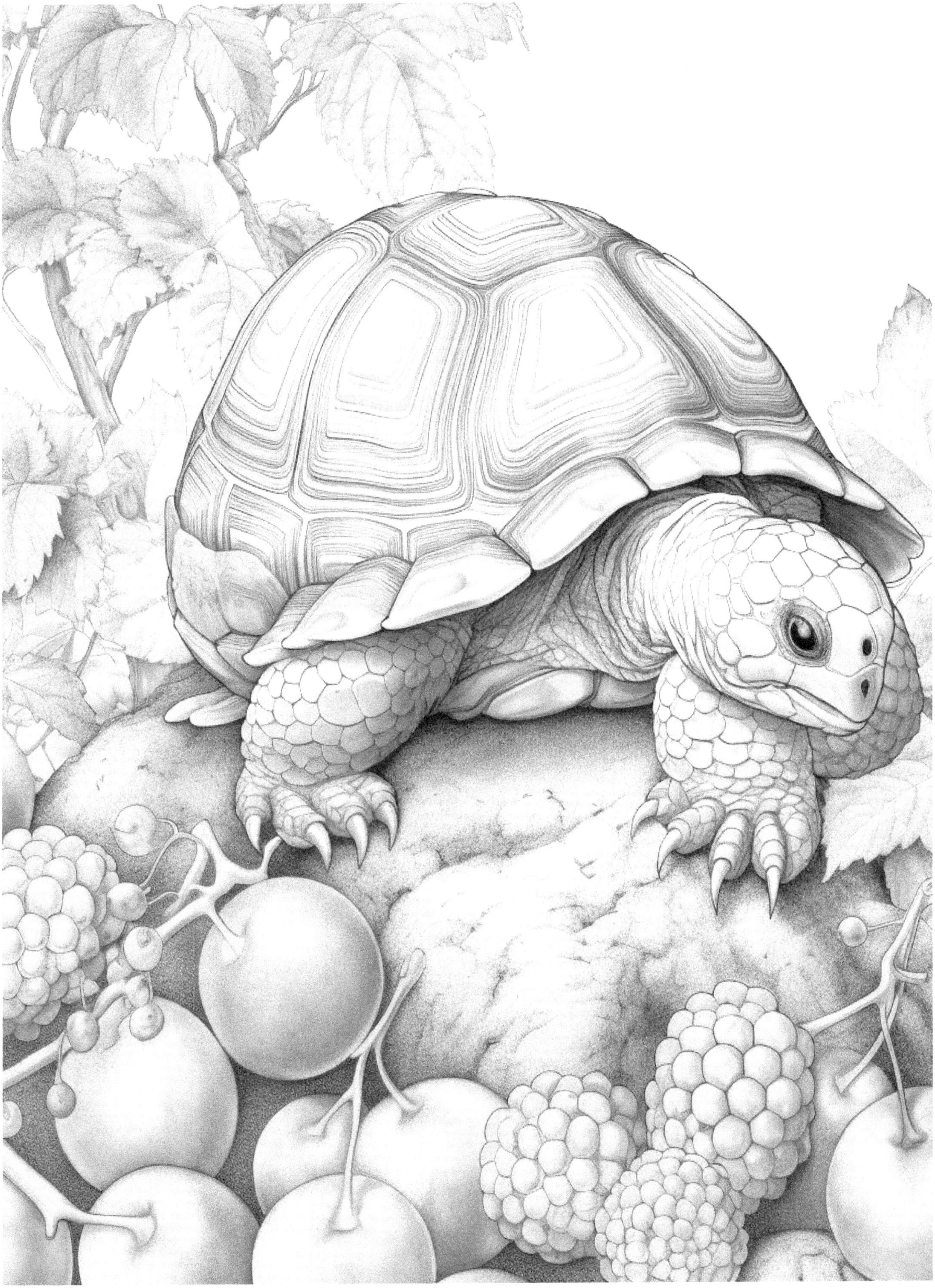

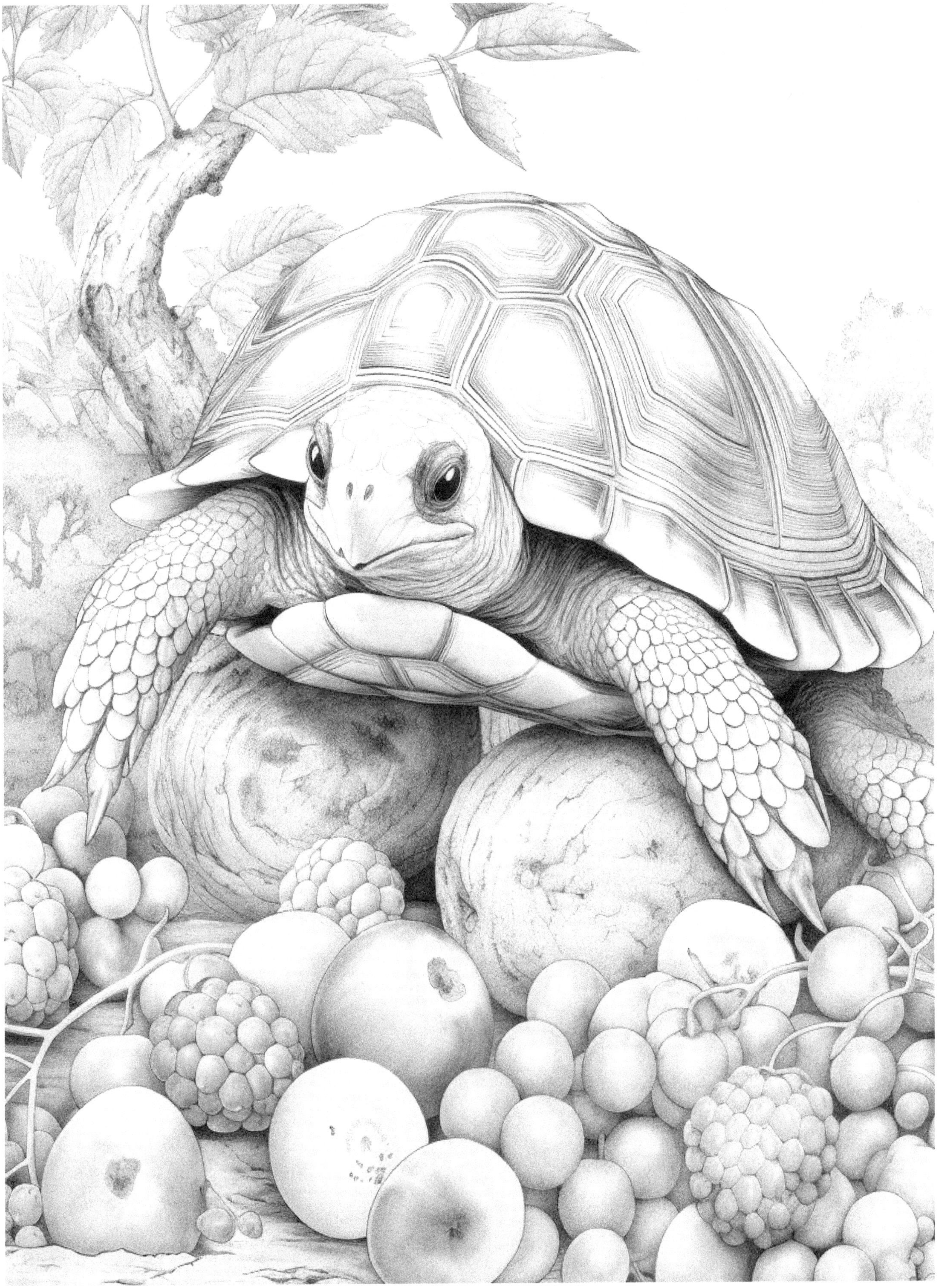

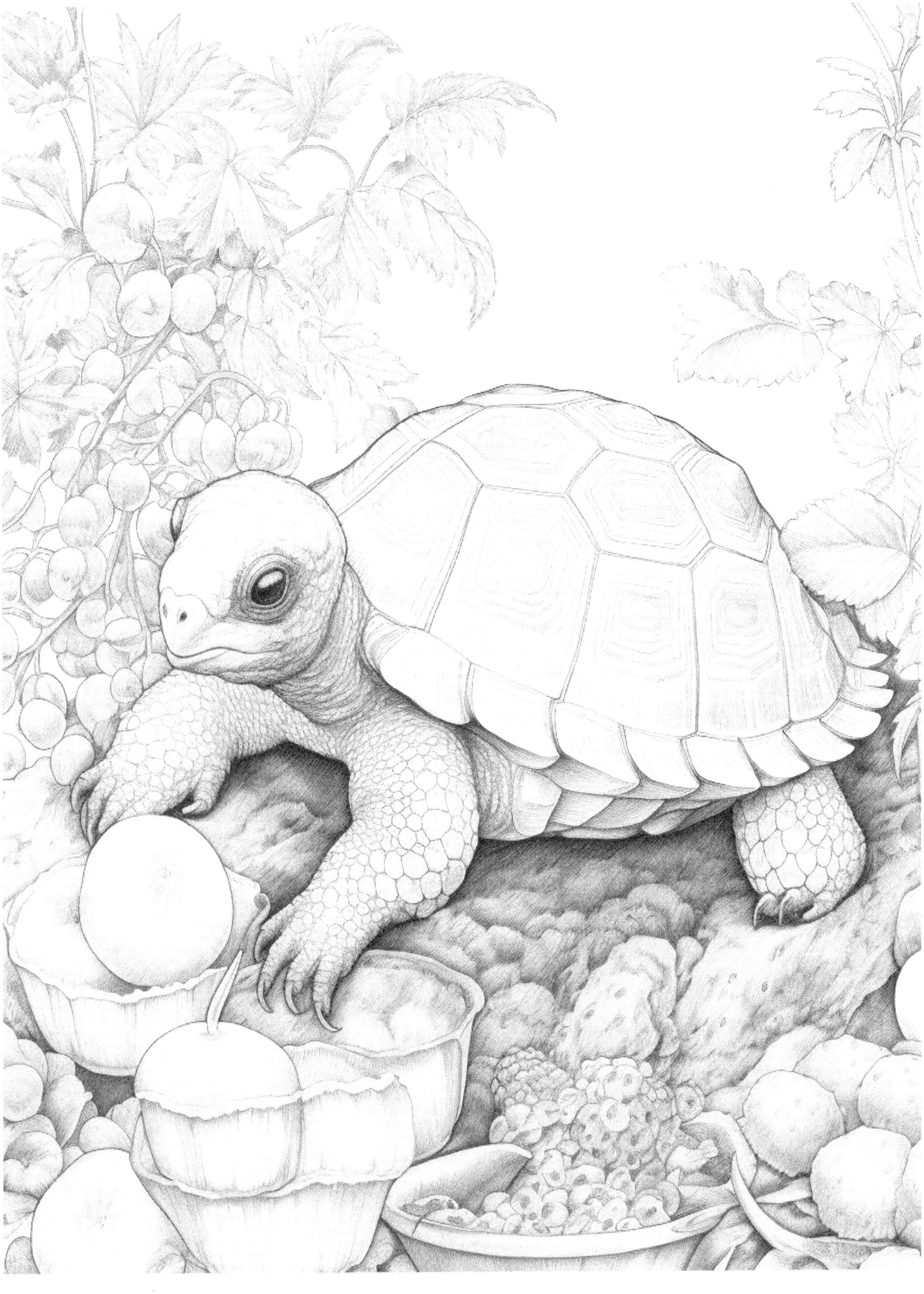

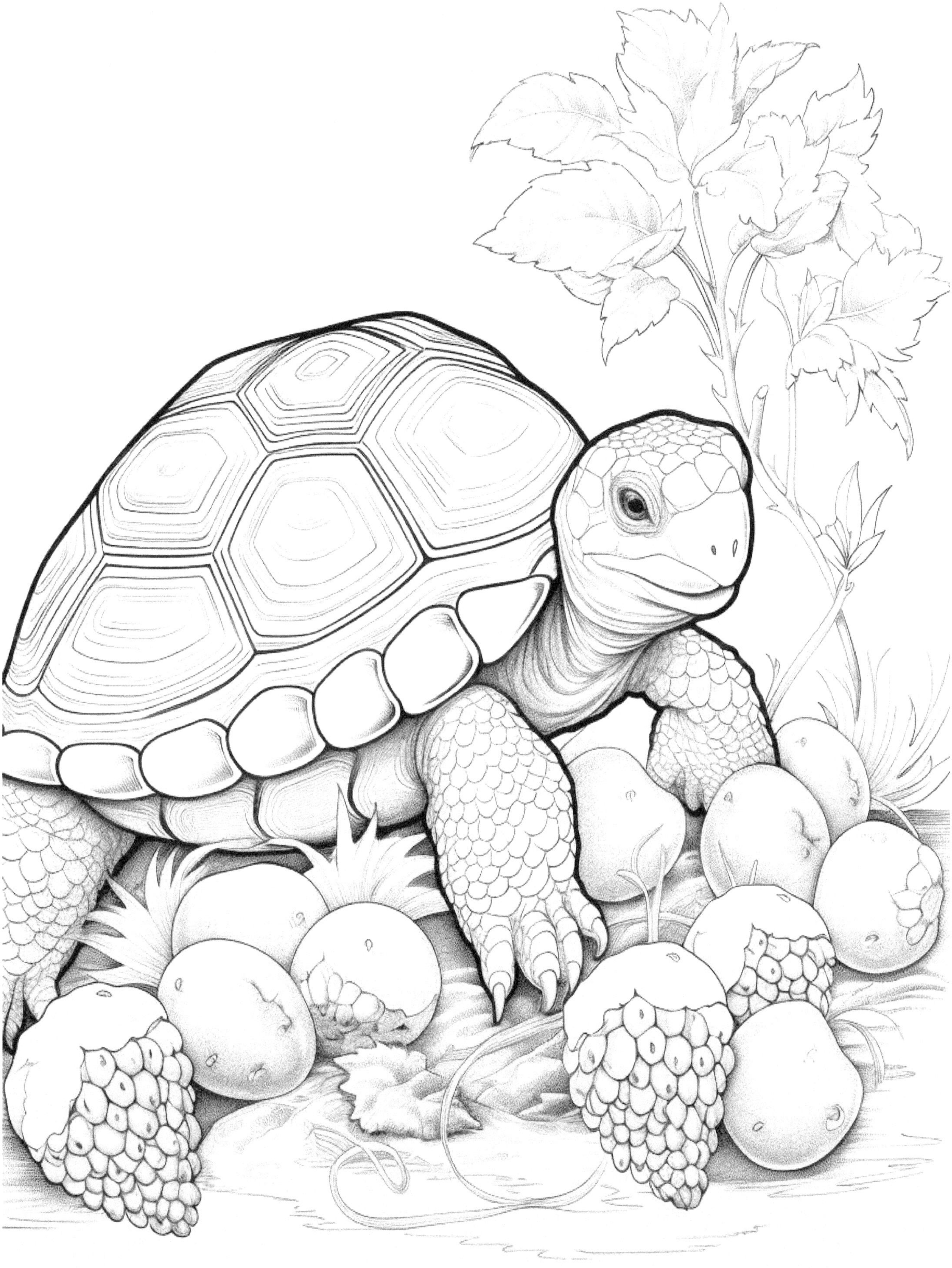

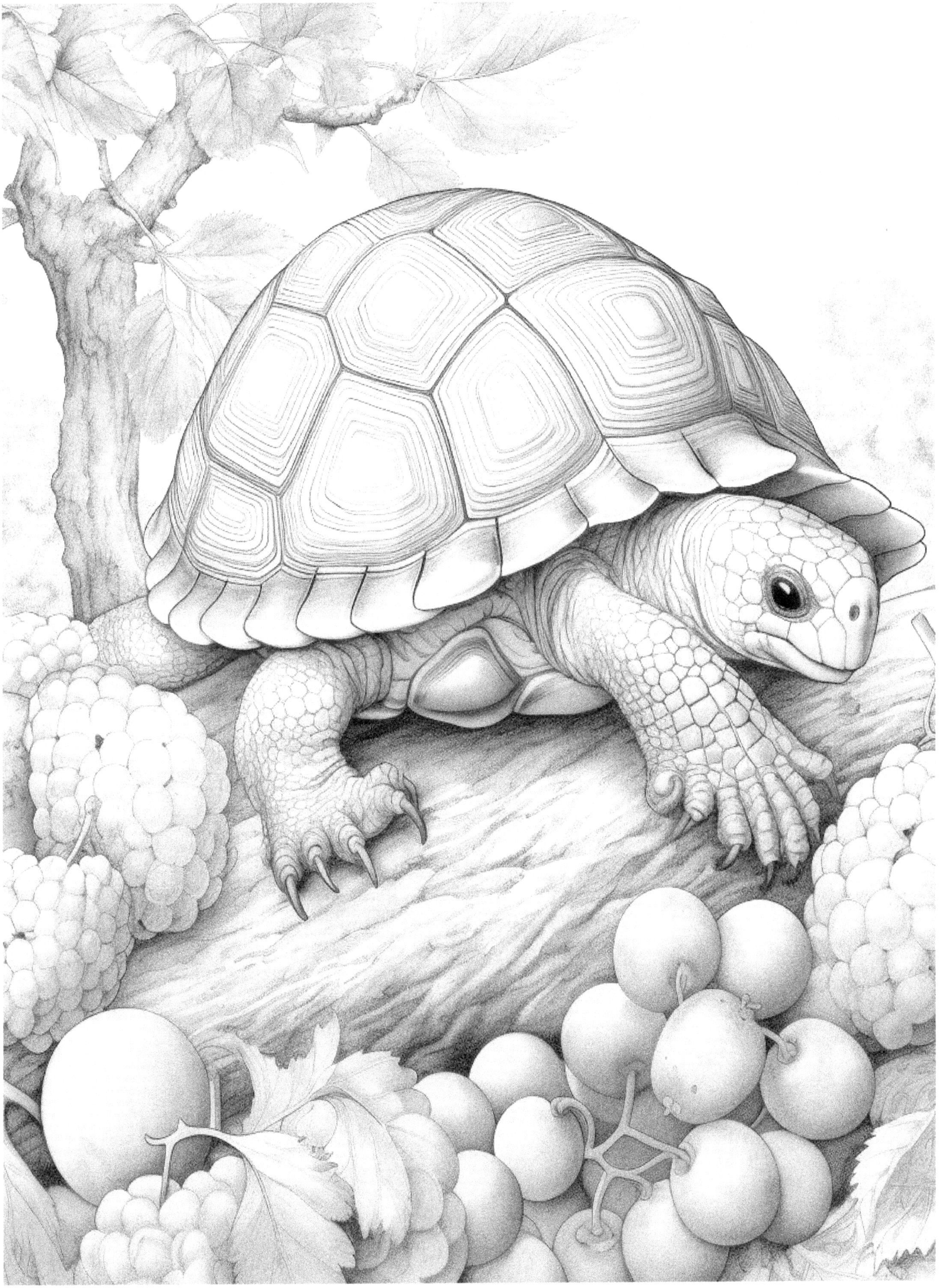

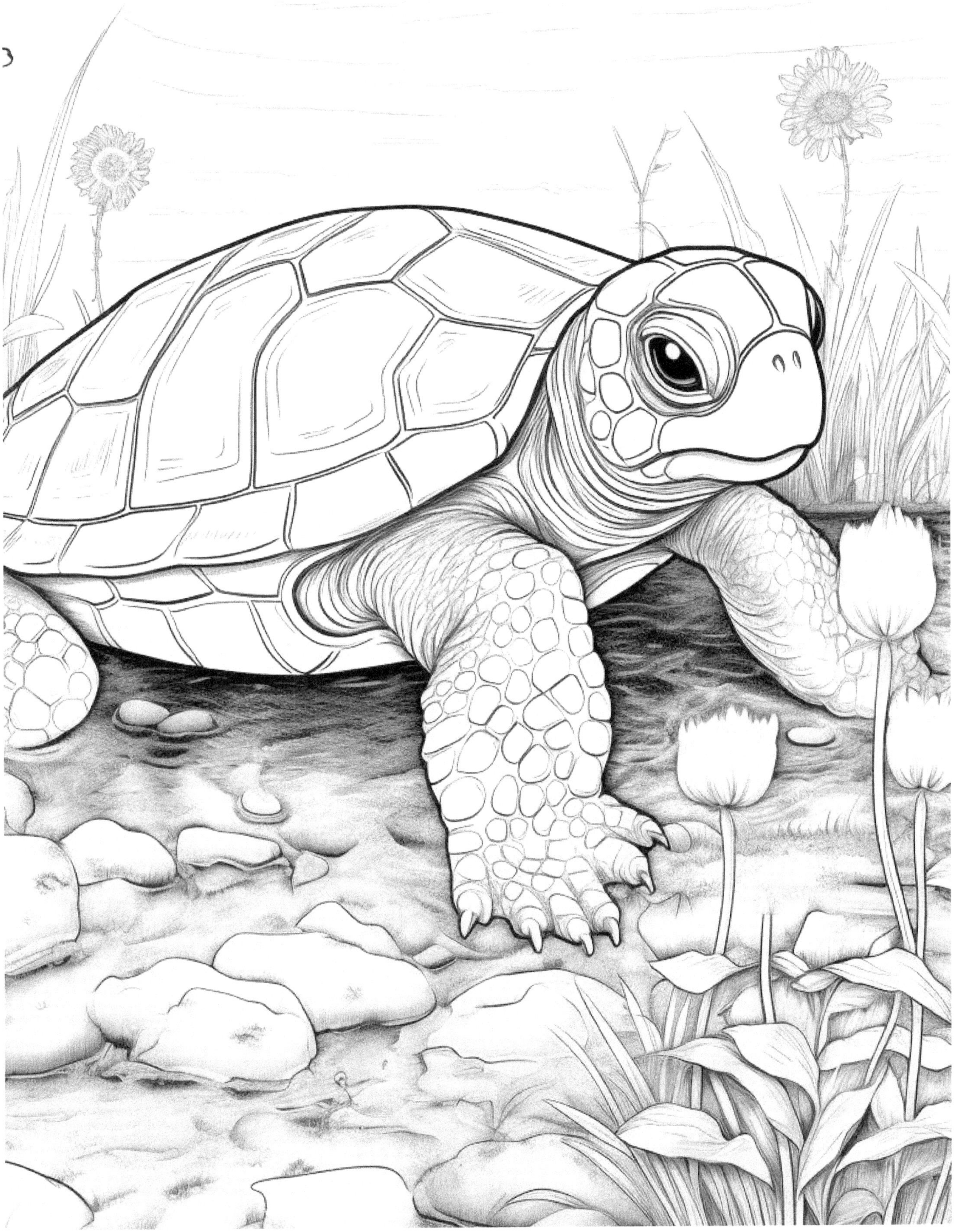

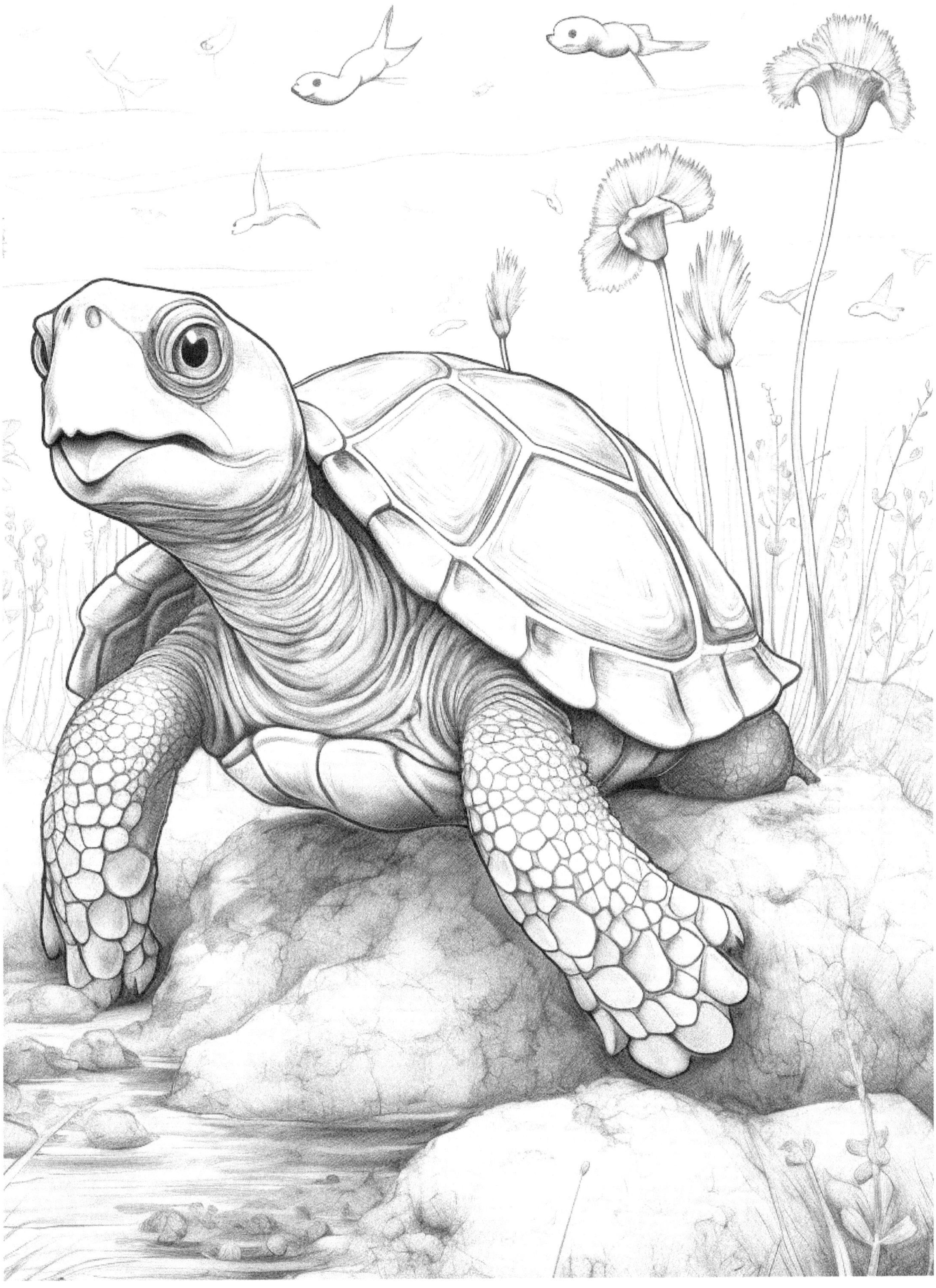

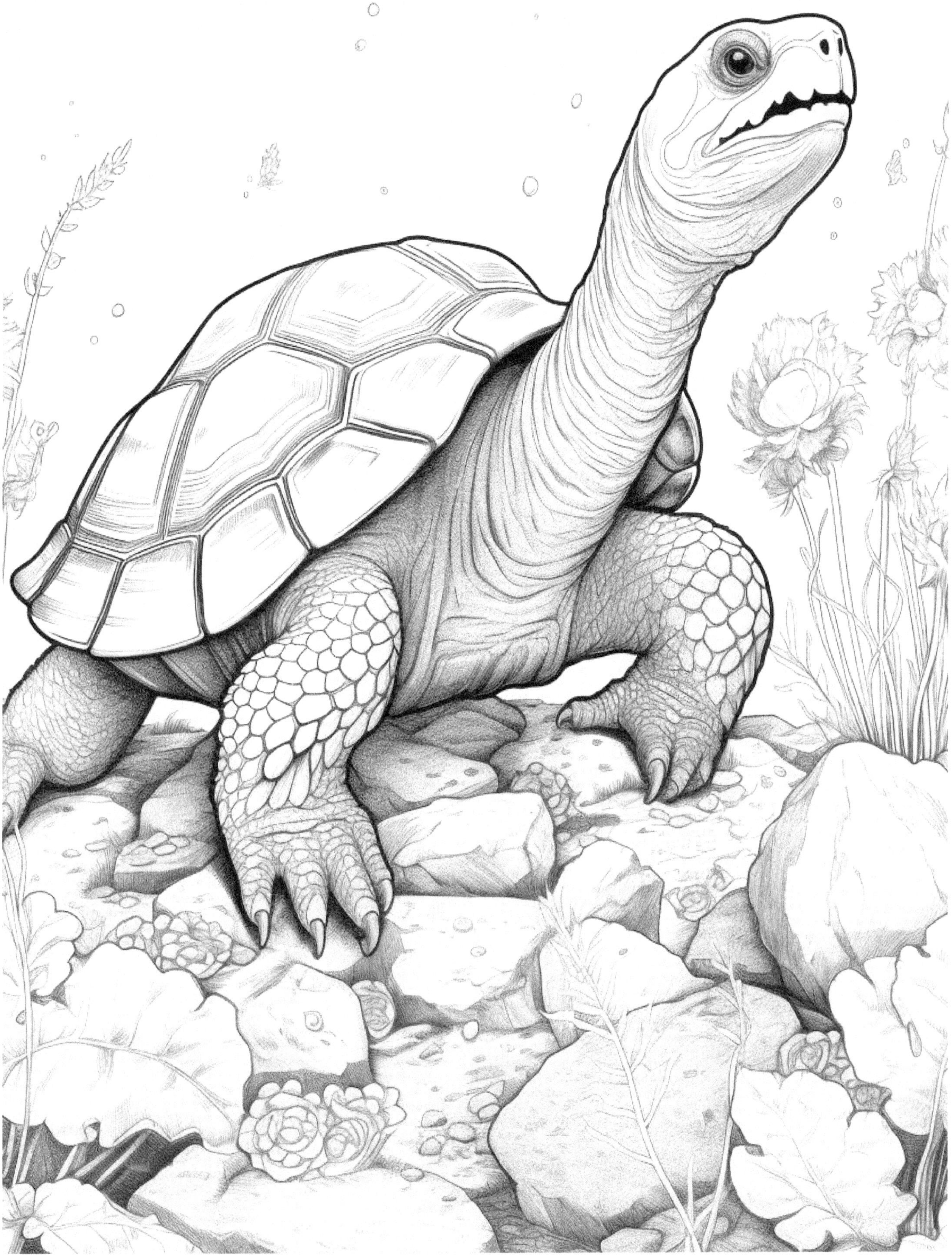

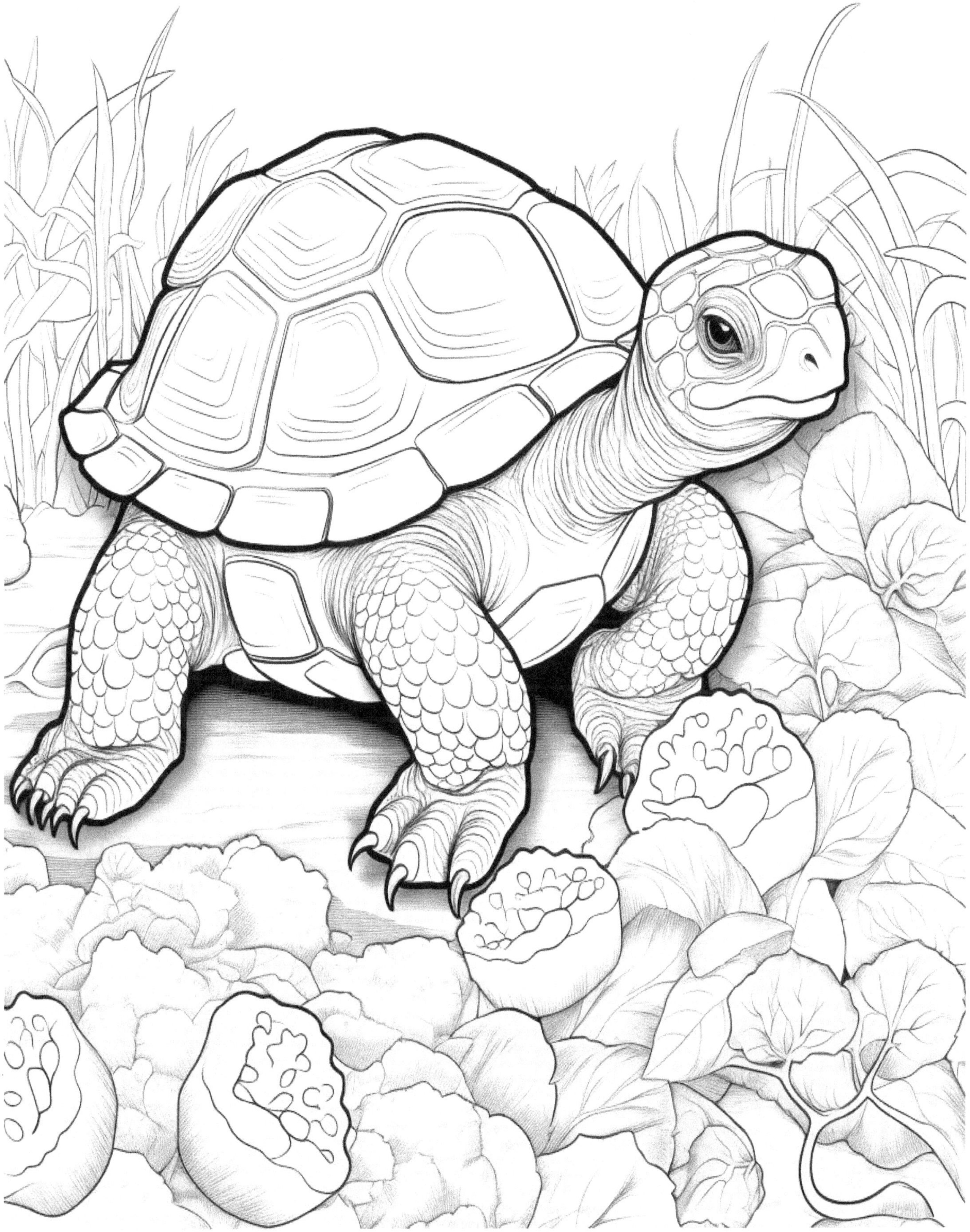

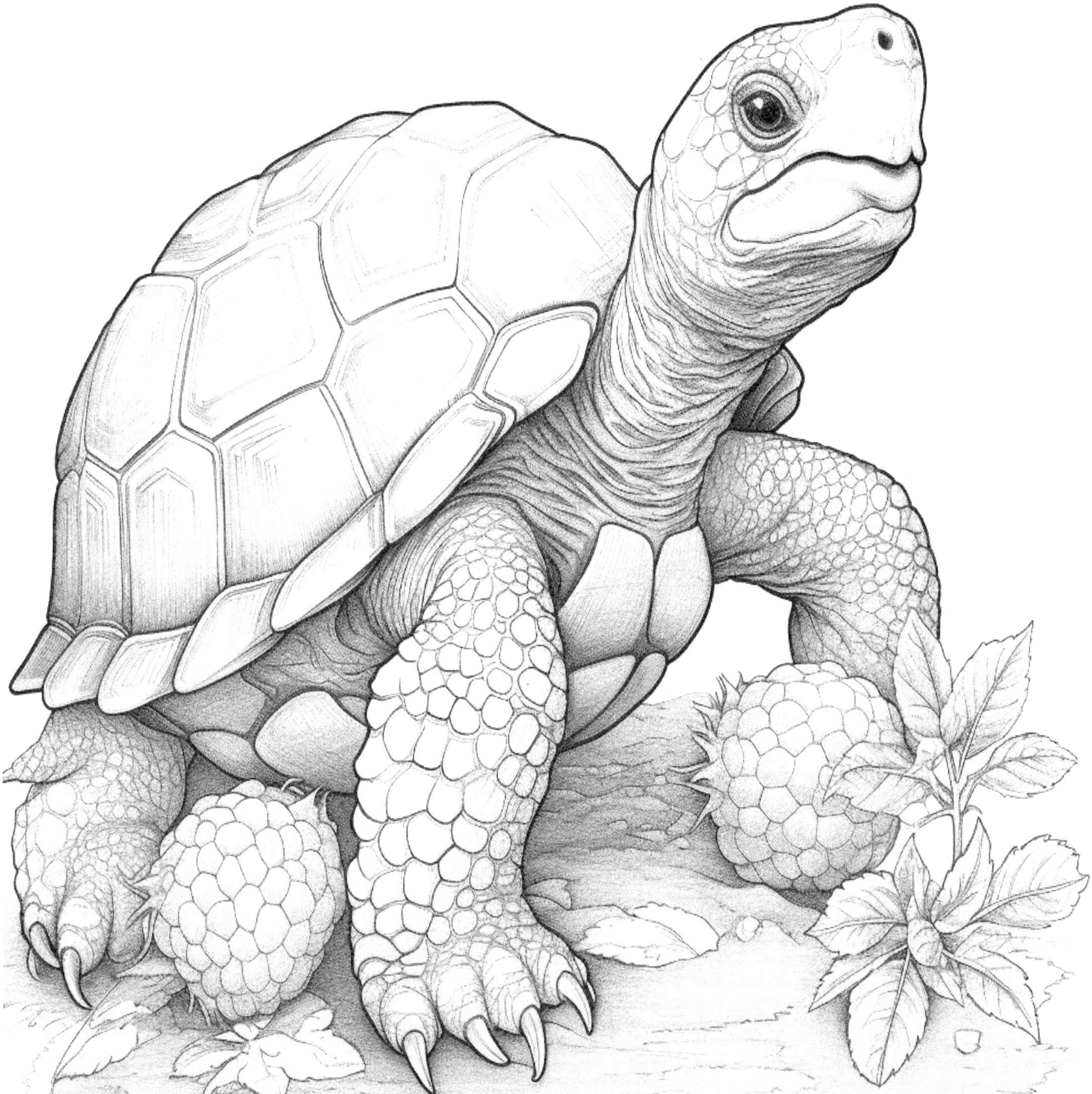

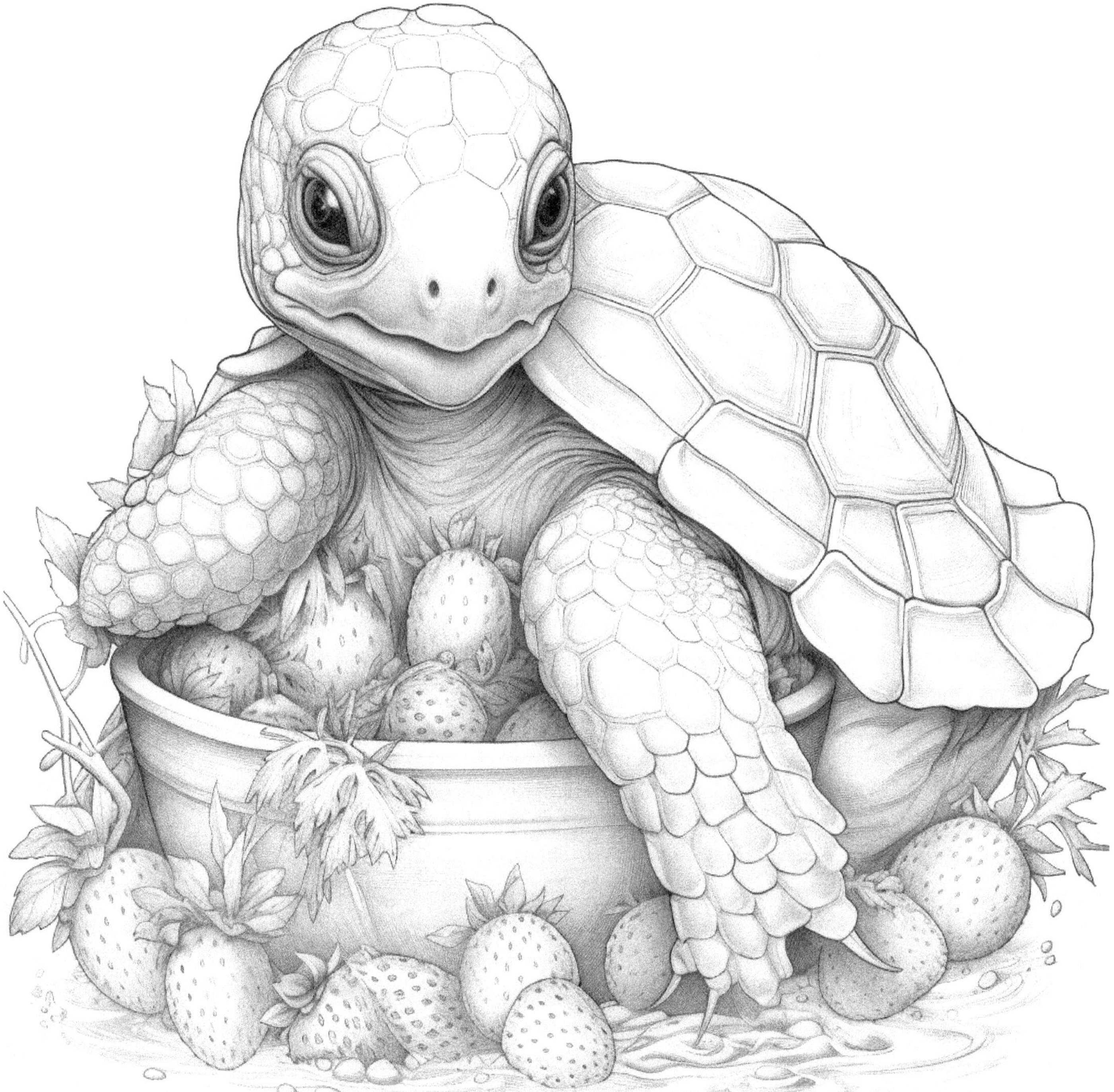

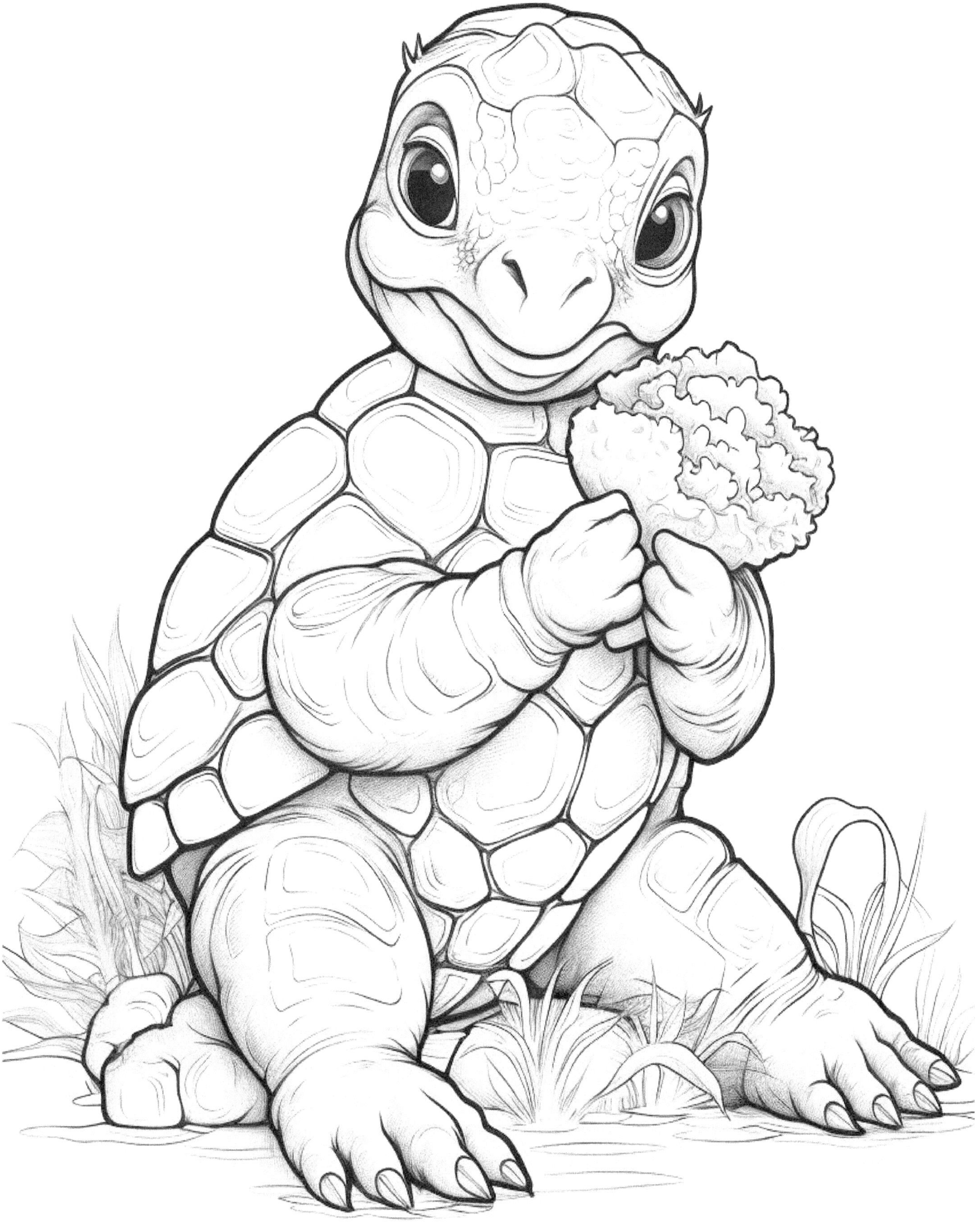

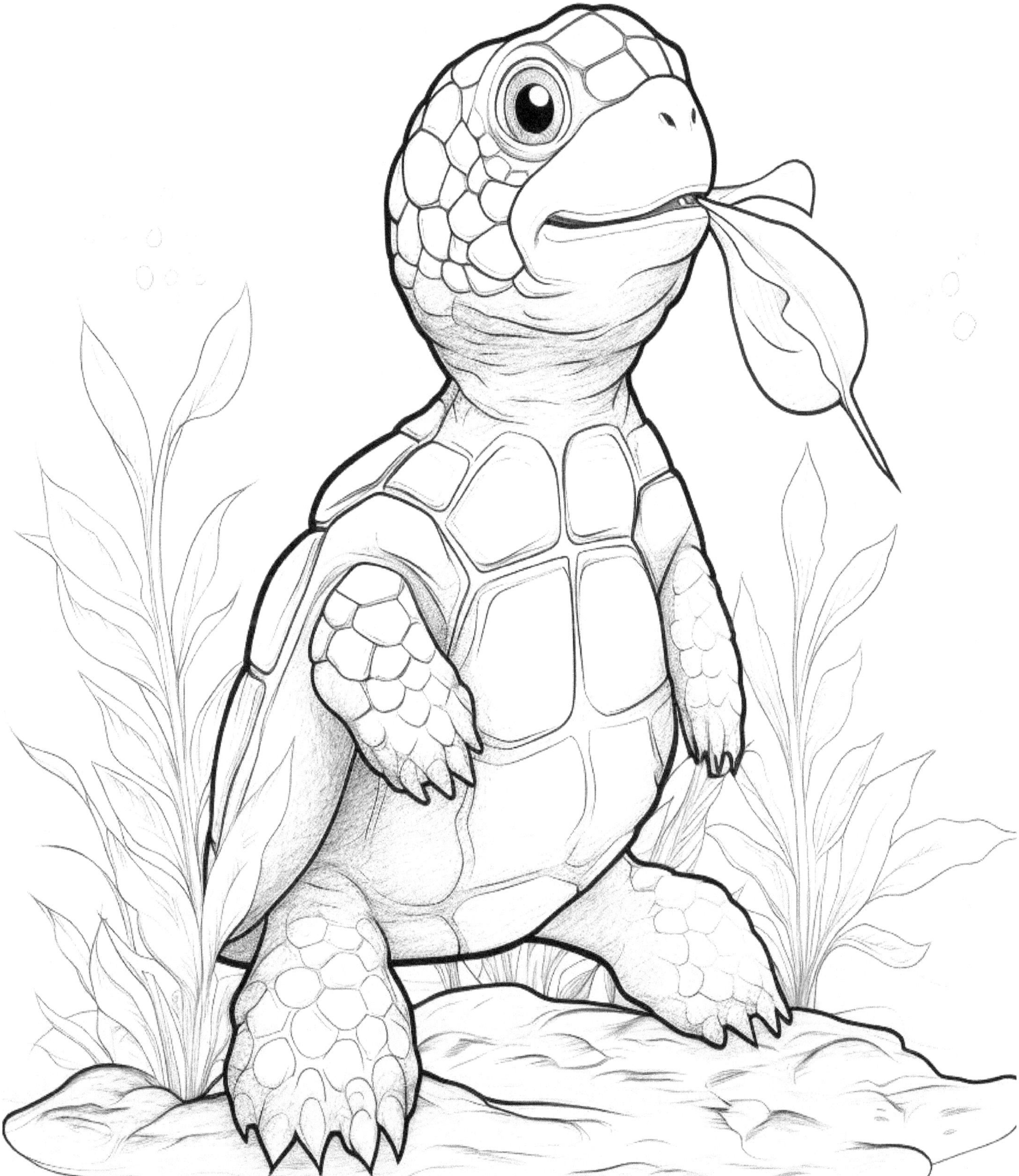

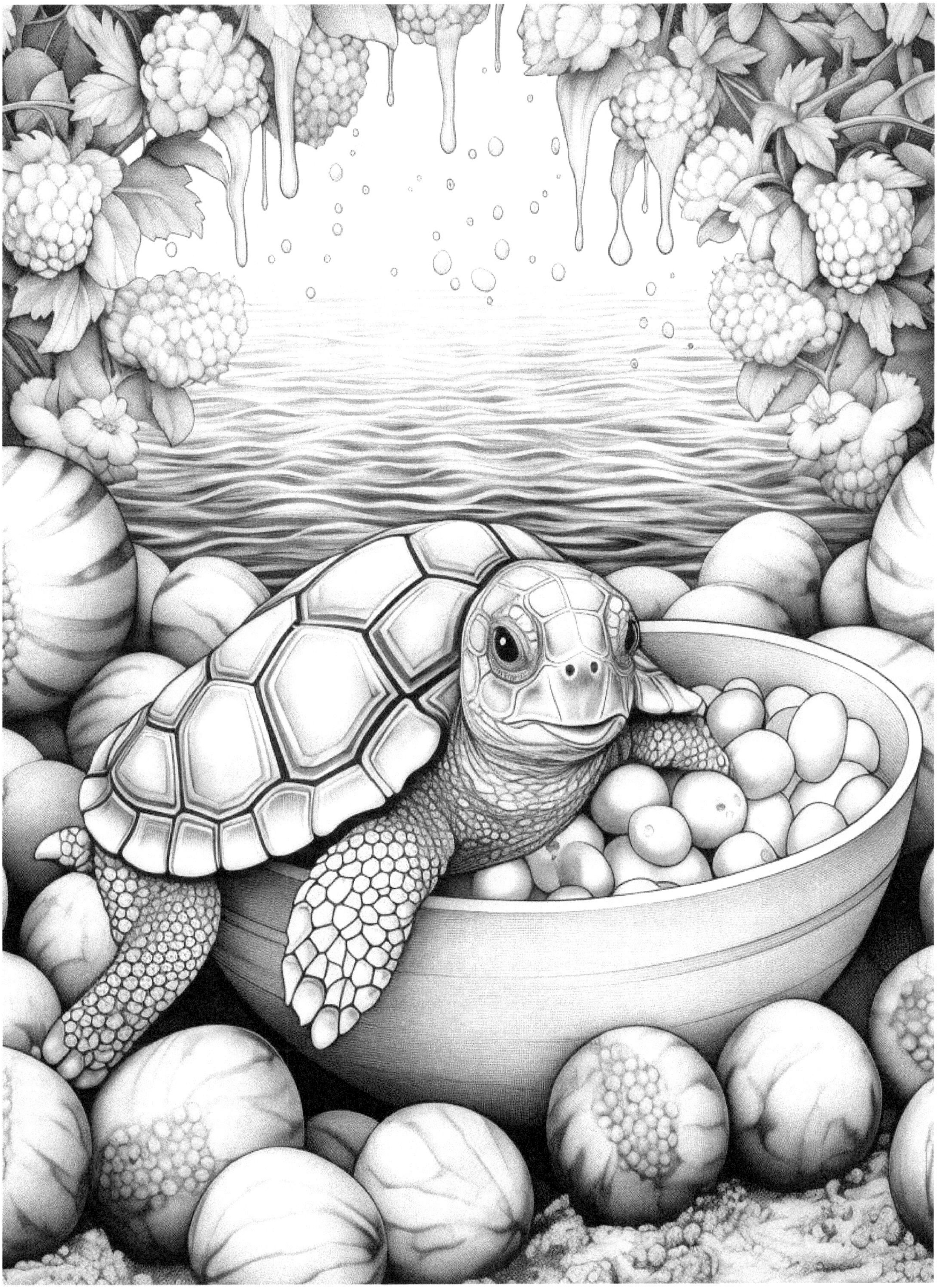

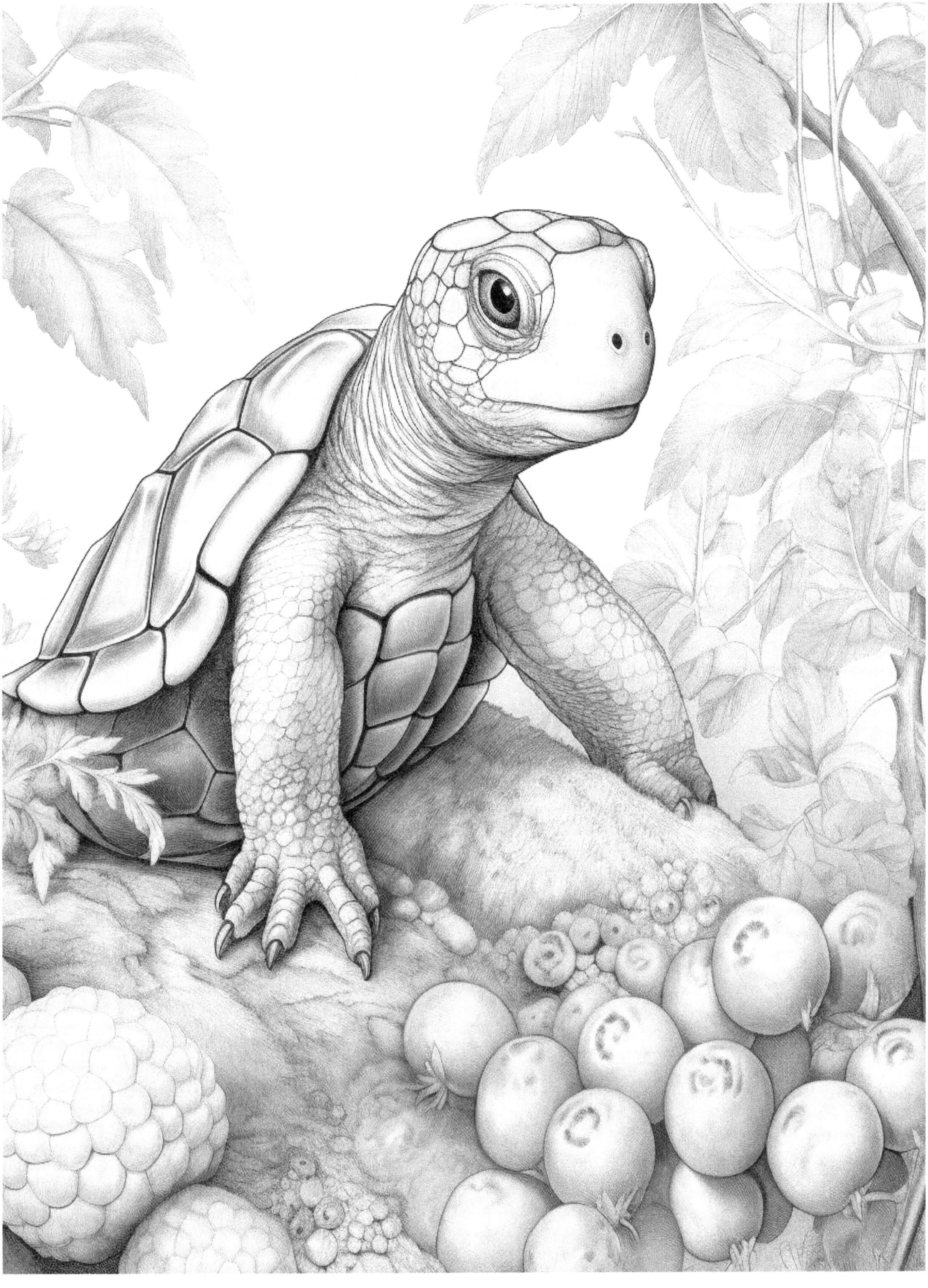

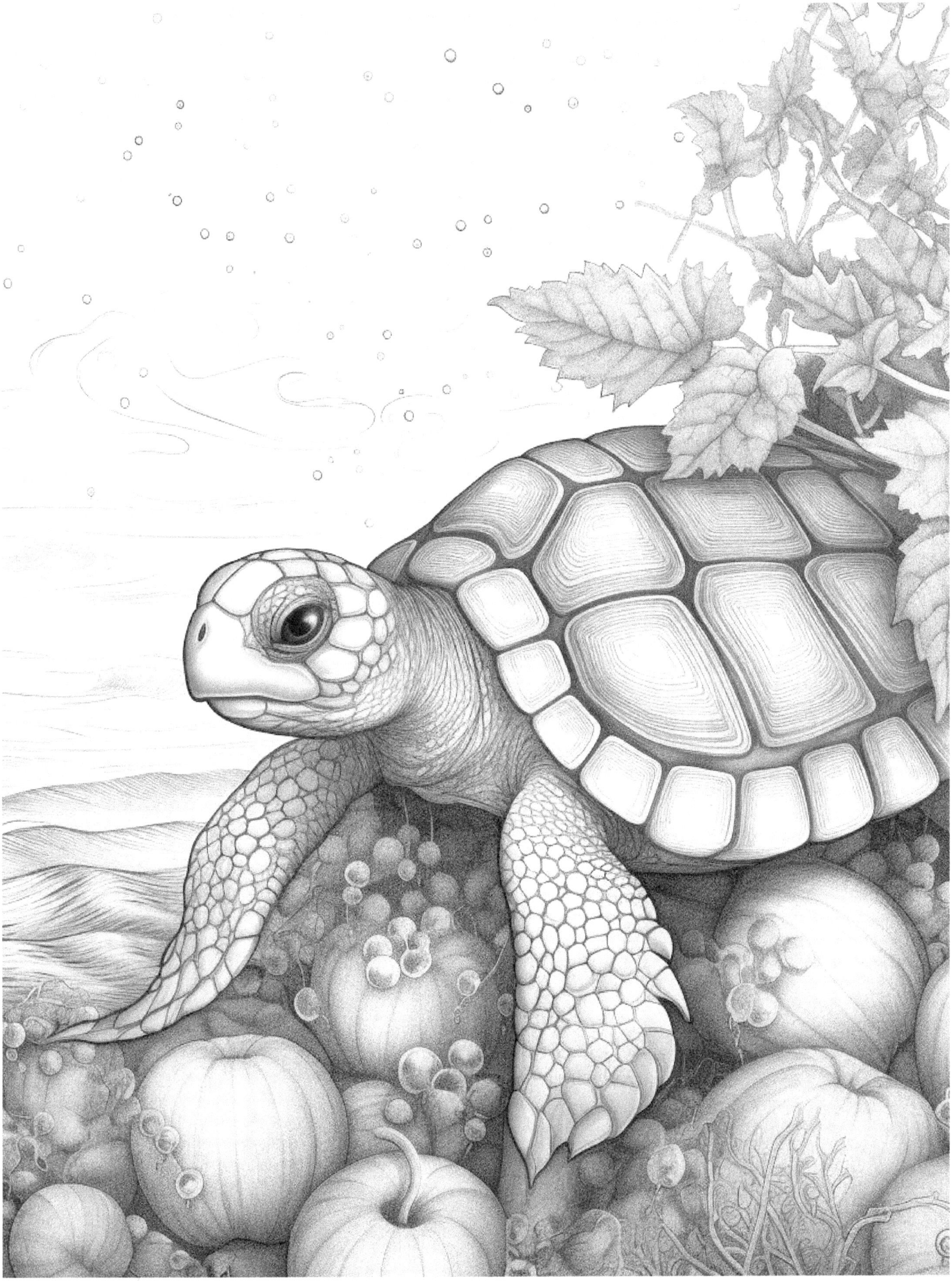

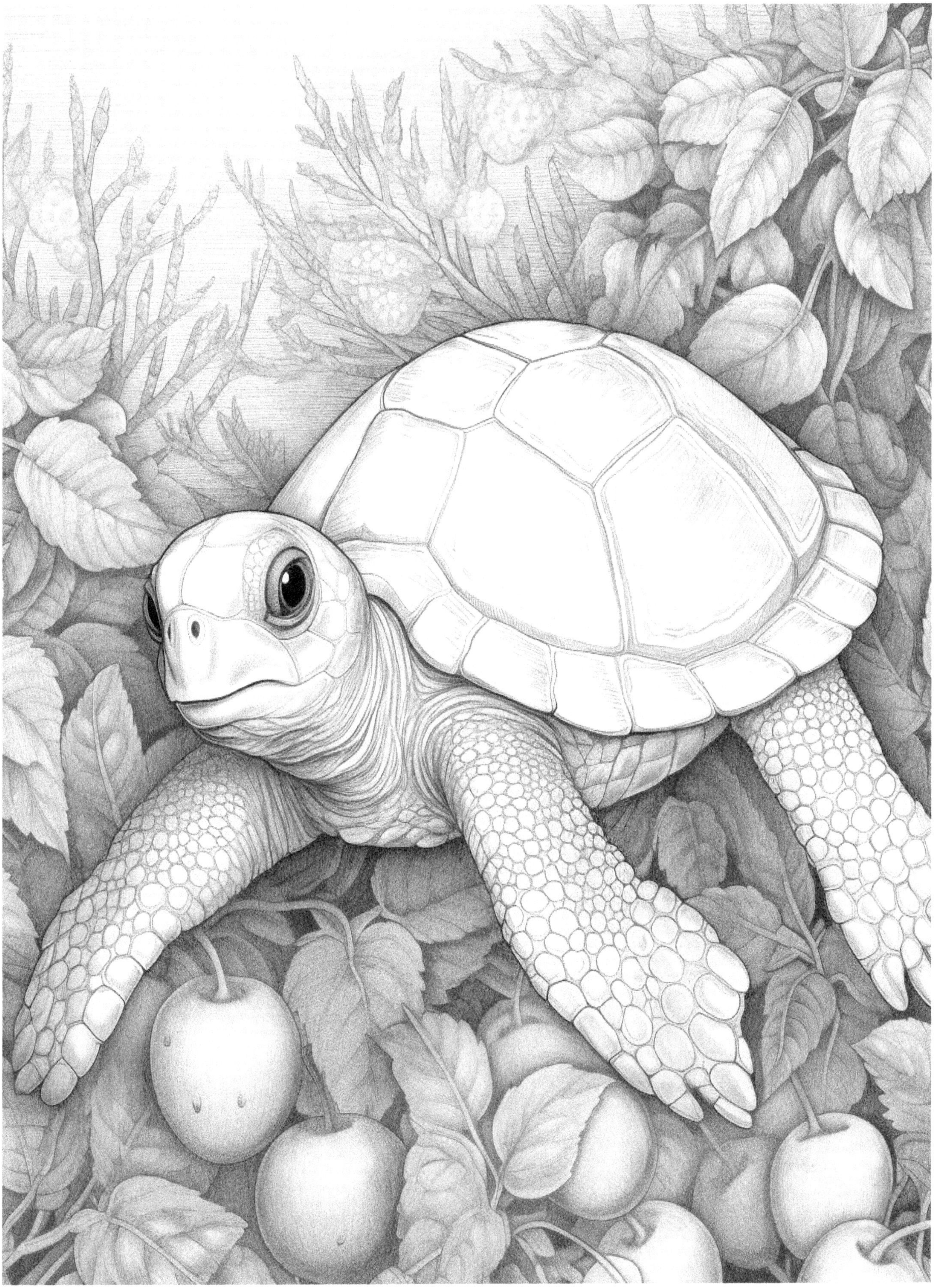

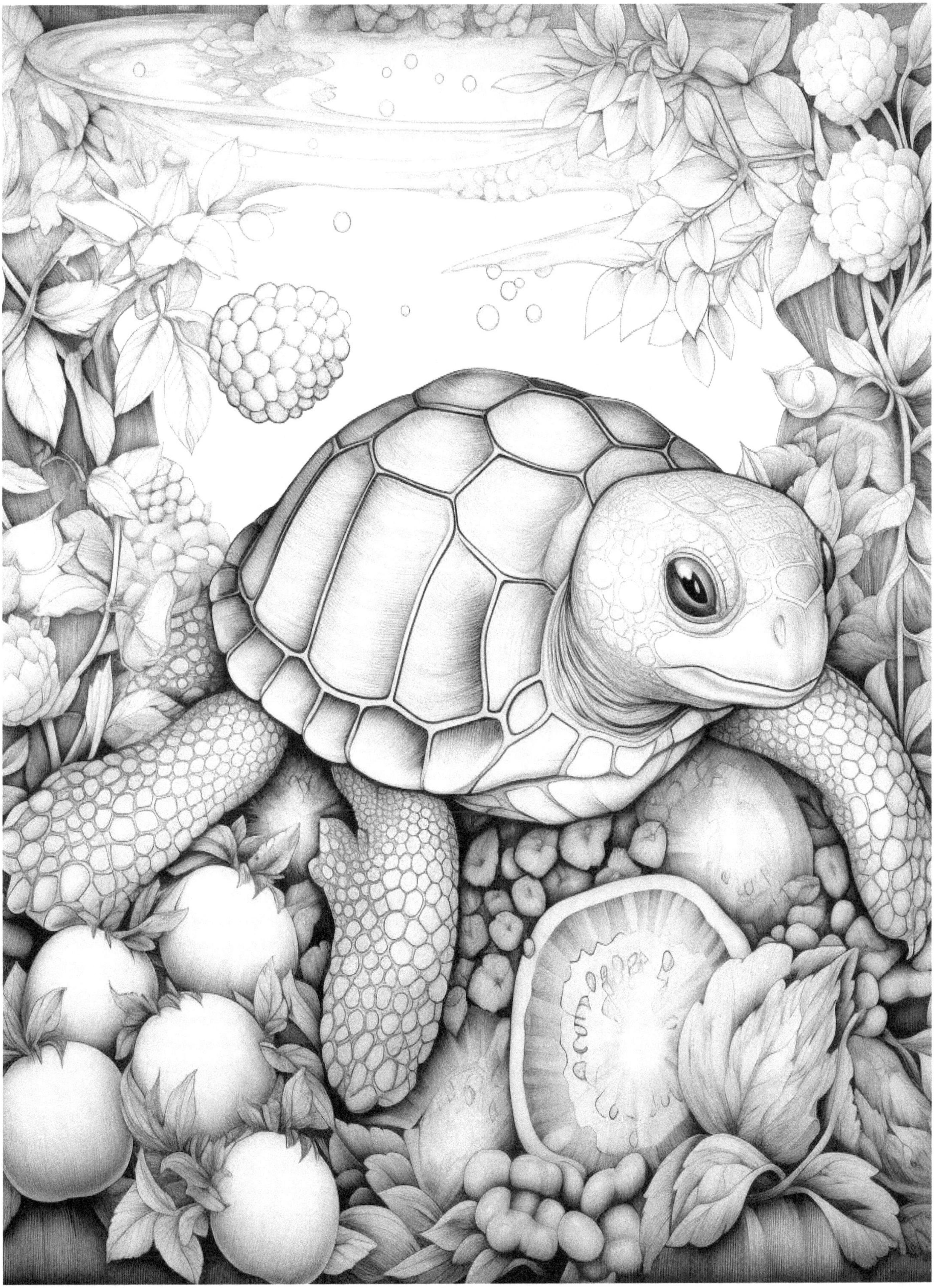

www.ingramcontent.com/pod-product-compliance
Lightning Source LLC
Chambersburg PA
CBHW080621220526
45466CB00010B/3419
9798394363092